Shiver

Declan Hughes

Methuen Drama

Published by Methuen Drama

1 3 5 7 9 10 8 6 4 2

First published in 2003 by
Methuen Publishing Limited,

Copyright © Declan Hughes 2003

Declan Hughes has asserted his right under the Copyright, Designs
and Patents Act, 1988, to be identified as the author of this work

A CIP catalogue record is available from the British Library

ISBN 0 413 77361 2

Typeset by SX Composing DTP, Rayleigh, Essex

ROUGH MAGIC PRESENTS THE WORLD PREMIÈRE OF

shiver

BY DECLAN HUGHES

ROUGH MAGIC PRESENTS THE WORLD PREMIÈRE OF

shiver

BY DECLAN HUGHES

CAST (IN ORDER OF SPEAKING)

RICHARD	**PETER HANLY**
JENNY	**CATHY WHITE**
MARION	**CATHY BELTON**
KEVIN	**PAUL HICKEY**

DIRECTOR	**LYNNE PARKER**
SET & LIGHTING DESIGNER	**JOHN COMISKEY**
COSTUME DESIGNER	**KATHY STRACHAN**
SOUND DESIGNER	**CORMAC CARROLL**
PRODUCTION MANAGER	**MARIE BREEN**
STAGE DIRECTOR	**PAULA TIERNEY**
STAGE MANAGER	**PAMELA McQUEEN**
PRODUCTION ELECTRICIAN	**BARRY CONWAY**
SET CONSTRUCTION	**THEATRE PRODUCTION SERVICES**
GRAPHIC DESIGN	**ALPHABET SOUP**
PRESS PUBLICIST	**SIOBHÁN COLGAN**
PRODUCER	**DEBORAH AYDON**

Rough Magic would like to thank the following for their kind assistance with this production: the Abbey Theatre, the Arts Council of Ireland, Declan Conlon, Derbhle Crotty, Dublin City Council, Seán Hillen, Ros Kavanagh, Moët Hennessy, Paula Shields, Gabrielle Stafford, and all the staff of Project Arts Centre.

The performance runs for approximately two hours, including one interval.

Shiver received its world première at Project Arts Centre, Dublin, on 28th March 2003.

Please note that the text of the play which appears in this volume may be changed during the rehearsal process and appear in slightly altered form in performance.

ROUGH MAGIC AND NEW WRITING

The core of Rough Magic's work is the development and production of new work for the stage. Founded in the mid-eighties, the company began by presenting Irish premières of major plays from the contemporary international scene, before beginning to commission and develop new plays from Irish writers. Declan Hughes's **I Can't Get Started** was one of the company's first commissions, and between its première at Dublin's Project Arts Centre in 1990 and the world première of **Shiver** at the same venue in 2003, our new writing programme has grown in scale, scope and depth.

Our Literary Department is always on the alert for exciting new work both in Ireland and overseas. A network of colleagues around the world means that we can stay abreast of developments in other countries and bring important work to Irish audiences. In 2002, for example, we produced the Irish première of Michael Frayn's extraordinary international hit, **Copenhagen** (Best Production, Irish Times/ESB Irish Theatre Awards), and presented **Scan:** public readings of new work from Scandinavia. We read, discuss and respond to the many scripts which are submitted for consideration, and provide feedback and encouragement to promising playwrights. And the Literary Manager works closely with our commissioned writers as they develop new plays for the company.

At any one time, our rolling programme of new play commissions includes a diverse range of work at various stages of development, and we currently have seven new pieces in progress for future production. Ioanna Anderson and Gerald Murphy are further developing the plays they wrote as part of our **Seeds** project. Arthur Riordan and Bell Helicopter are collaborating on **Improbable Frequency**, a new piece of music theatre. Elizabeth Kuti is writing a new play exploring sexual politics and political morality among the Quaker community in nineteenth-century Dublin. Ali White and Hélène Montague are working on a stage adaptation, with music, of Tynyanov's **Lieutenant Kijé**. And both Oonagh Kearney and Gina Moxley are about to start work on new plays for the company.

Seeds, a new play initiative created by Rough Magic and the Dublin Fringe Festival, was established in 2001 to seek out, encourage, enable, develop and stage new Irish writing. After a painstaking selection process, six emerging writers were chosen for commission, and each was supported by workshops and private readings, and assigned a mentor from a group of highly experienced international directors. The six resulting plays were presented as public readings in 2002, and a high proportion are being developed towards production. We are now working towards a new cycle of **Seeds**, beginning in 2004.

This tradition of encouraging new talent is a long-standing one, and Declan Hughes is just one of many writers who began their careers with the company and have gone on to write for the major stages in Ireland and the UK. Like Declan, many also remain part of the Rough Magic stable. Eight debut plays commissioned and produced by the company in the 80's and 90's were recently published by New Island Books in the single volume **Rough Magic: First Plays**, and the most recent Rough Magic debut was Morna Regan's **Midden**, which toured Ireland between its Edinburgh festival première and its London season at Hampstead Theatre, picking up a number of awards on the way.

As the company approaches its twentieth anniversary, we aim to expand this new writing programme, to stage more of the exciting new work which has built Rough Magic's reputation, and to extend the international focus of our work. Above all, we plan to remain true to our belief that new writing is the lifeblood of our theatre.

Further information on Rough Magic is regularly updated at **www.rough-magic.com.**

DECLAN HUGHES WRITER

Declan is co-founder of Rough Magic. He was originally joint Artistic Director, before becoming Writer-in-Residence for several years, and is now an Associate Artist of the company. His writing for Rough Magic includes **I Can't Get Started** (Project, Edinburgh Festival Fringe and Stoneybrook International Festival, New York 1990/91, winner of the Stewart Parker Trust Award); an adaptation of Farquhar's **Love and a Bottle** (Project, national tour, Glasgow Mayfest and Tricycle Theatre 1992, joint winner of Time Out Best Play Award); **Digging For Fire** (Project, national tour and Bush Theatre 1992, joint winner of Time Out Best Play Award); **New Morning** (Rough Magic/Bush co-production, Bush Theatre and Project 1993), and **Halloween Night** (Andrews Lane and Donmar Warehouse 1997). Other work for the stage includes **Twenty Grand** at the Peacock in 1998 and an adaptation of Molière's **Tartuffe** for the Abbey Theatre in 2000.

Film and television writing includes **Gallows Thief, The Flying Scotsman, Another Life, Younger than Springtime, My Friend Joe** (winner of the Golden Bear Award, Berlin Film Festival) and the RTE/BBC short film **Career Opportunities.**

LYNNE PARKER DIRECTOR

Lynne is co-founder and Artistic Director of Rough Magic Theatre Company and an Associate Director of the Abbey Theatre.

Productions for Rough Magic include **Top Gi s, Decadence, The Country Wife, Nightshade, Spokesong, Serious Money, Aunt Dan and Lemon, The Tempest, Tom and Viv, Lady Windermere's Fan, Digging For Fire, Love And A Bottle, I Can't Get Started, New Morning, Danti Dan, Down Onto Blue, The Dogs, Hidden Charges, Halloween Night, The Way Of The World, Pentecost, Northern Star, The School for Scandal, The Whisperers, Boomtown, Three Days Of Rain, Dead Funny, Midden** and **Copenhagen** (Best Production, Irish Times/ESB Irish Theatre Awards).

Productions at the Abbey and Peacock theatres include **The Trojan Women, The Doctor's Dilemma, Tartuffe, Down the Line, The Sanctuary Lamp** and **The Drawer Boy** (Galway Arts Festival co-production).

Other work outside the company includes productions for Druid, Tinderbox, Opera Theatre Company and 7:84 Scotland, and Lynne was an associate artist of Charabanc for whom she adapted and directed **The House of Bernarda Alba.** Lynne has also directed **The Clearing** (Bush Theatre); **The Playboy of the Western World, The Silver Tassie** and **Our Father** (Almeida Theatre); **Brothers of the Brush** (Arts Theatre); **The Shadow of a Gunman** (Gate, Dublin); **Playhouse Creatures** (The Peter Hall Company at the Old Vic); **The Importance of Being Earnest** (West Yorkshire Playhouse); **Love Me?!** (Corn Exchange's Car Show); **The Comedy of Errors** (RSC) and **Olga** (Traverse Theatre, Edinburgh).

CATHY BELTON MARION

This is Cathy's first appearance in a Rough Magic production. Her theatre credits include **Stolen Child** (Calypso Theatre Company); **Women in Arms** and **Silas Marner** (Storytellers Theatre Company); **The Plough and the Stars, Whistle in the Dark, Playboy of the Western World, Tartuffe, Medea, Living Quarters, The Broken Jug, A Crucial Week in the Life of a Grocer's Assistant** and **Silverlands** (Abbey/Peacock theatres); **Hamlet** (Loose Canon); **An Triall, Milseog an tSamhraidh, Fear an Tae,** (Amharclann de hÍde); **Kitchensink** and **Buddleia** (Passion Machine); **Hamlet, The Tempest, Romeo and Juliet** and **The Conquest of the South Pole** (Island Theatre Company), and **True Lines** (Bickerstaffe Theatre Company).

Film and television work includes **Fergus's Wedding, Tubberware, Paths to Freedom, Trí Sceal, First Communion Day, Racing Homer, Before I Sleep, Circle of Friends, Glenroe, Making the Cut, House at Jerusalem** and **The Snapper.**

PETER HANLY RICHARD

Peter has previously appeared with Rough Magic in **Three Days of Rain, The School for Scandal, Down Onto Blue, The Way of the World** and **Digging For Fire.** He was a member of Dublin Youth Theatre before joining Theatre Unlimited, where he worked as a company member for two years. Other theatre credits include **Taste** (Gúna Nua Theatre Company); **Communion, Big Maggie** and **Sive** (Abbey/Peacock theatres); **Kvetch** (Kilkenny Arts Festival); **The Promise** and **The Lonesome West** (Liverpool Everyman); **Making Noise Quietly** (Oxford Stage Company); **Love Me?!** (Corn Exchange's Car Show); **The Gay Detective** (Project and Tricycle Theatre); **The Seagull** and **The Breadman** (Gate Theatre); **Lovechild** (Project); **The Ash Fire** (Pigsback Theatre Company, Project and Tricycle); **The Conquest of the South Pole** (Theatre Demo); **A Life** (Olympia Theatre); **Translations** and **Bent** (Red Kettle Theatre Company).

Peter's film and television work includes **Black Day at Black Rock, Ballykissangel, First Communion Day, Jumpers!, Guiltrip, Braveheart,** and **The Truth About Claire.** He has also recorded several radio plays with both RTE and BBC.

PAUL HICKEY KEVIN

Paul has previously appeared with Rough Magic in **Halloween Night, Pentecost, Lady Windermere's Fan** and **Spokesong.** Other theatre credits include **Crazyblackmuthafuckin'self** (Royal Court); **Dealer's Choice** and **My Night With Reg** (Birmingham Rep); **The Merchant of Venice** (Royal Shakespeare Company); **Peer Gynt, Romeo and Juliet** and **The Playboy of the Western World** (National Theatre); **Drink, Dance, Laugh and Lie** (Bush Theatre); **Love Me?!** (Corn Exchange's Car Show); **In a Little World of Our Own** (Donmar Warehouse); **Deep Blue Sea** (Royal Exchange); **Red Roses and Petrol, The Ash Fire, Howling Moons Silent Sons** and **The Tender Trap** (Pigsback Theatre Company, which he co-founded); and **The Plough and the Stars** and **The Silver Tassie** (Abbey).

Film and television credits include **Spin the Bottle, On The Edge, Though the Sky Falls, Nora, Ordinary Decent Criminal, The General, The American, Saving Private Ryan, The Matchmaker, Moll Flanders, Rebel Heart, Father Ted, The Informant, The Governor** and **Nighthawks.**

CATHY WHITE JENNY

This is Cathy's first appearance with Rough Magic. Theatre credits include **Blackwater Angel, The Barbaric Comedies, As The Beast Sleeps, Tarry Flynn** and **The Trojan Women** (Abbey/Peacock theatres); **Force of Change** and **The Weir** (Royal Court); **Stone and Ashes** (Dublin Theatre Festival); **Dancing at Lughnasa** (Lyric Theatre, Belfast) and in England, seasons with the Royal Shakespeare Company, Royal National Theatre, Cheek By Jowl and at Manchester's Royal Exchange.

Film and television work includes the forthcoming **Murphy's Law, On Home Ground, The Cry, Perfect, Vicious Circle, Titanic Town, Saoirse, Night Train, The General, Snakes and Ladders, Nothing Personal, Grushko, The Big O** and **The Buddha of Suburbia.**

DEBORAH AYDON PRODUCER

As Executive Producer of Rough Magic, Deborah has produced **Copenhagen, Scan, Midden, Dead Funny, Plays⁴, Three Days of Rain, Boomtown** and **The Whisperers,** and acted as Project Manager on the company's site-specific temporary theatre for the 1999 Dublin Theatre Festival. Deborah arrived at Rough Magic after eight years as General Manager and Executive Producer of London's Bush Theatre. Aside from Rough Magic's visits with Declan Hughes's **Digging for Fire** and **New Morning** (a Bush co-production), highlights of this period include Billy Roche's **Wexford Trilogy** (also Peacock Theatre); Jonathan Harvey's **Beautiful Thing** (also national tour, Donmar and Duke of Yorks); Tracy Letts's **Killer Joe** (also West End); Joe Penhall's **Love and Understanding** (also Long Wharf Theater, New Haven, Connecticut); Conor McPherson's **This Lime Tree Bower** and **St Nicholas** (also New York), and Mark O'Rowe's **Howie the Rookie** (also Civic Theatre Tallaght and Andrews Lane).

MARIE BREEN PRODUCTION MANAGER

Marie has previously worked with Rough Magic on **Copenhagen, Dead Funny, Pentecost, The Whisperers** and **The School for Scandal**. Other recent work includes the Dublin Theatre Festival 2002, the first International Dance Festival 2002; **The Book of Evidence** (Kilkenny Arts Festival/Fiach Mac Conghail); **My Brilliant Divorce** (Druid); **The Silver Tassie, The Flying Dutchman, Lady Macbeth of Mtsensk** and **Madama Butterfly** (all Opera Ireland); **Peeling Venus** and **The Salt Cycle** (Rex Levitates); **Macbeth, Romeo and Juliet** and **King Lear** (Second Age); **Equivalents** (Temenos Project); **Oedipus** (Storytellers); **The Flowerbed** (Fabulous Beast) and **L'Altro Mondo** (Opera Machine).

JOHN COMISKEY SET AND LIGHTING DESIGNER

John has previously worked with Rough Magic on **Copenhagen** (for which he won Best Set Designer in the Irish Times/ESB Irish Theatre Awards), **Three Days of Rain, Pentecost, The Way of the World, Love and a Bottle** and **The Country Wife.** Other lighting designs include productions for the Abbey, Druid, Daghdha, Siamsa Tire, Project, and the dance/jewellery installation, **Lifecycles,** at the Crafts Council. John co-devised and directed **The Well** at the Dublin Theatre Festival 2000 and Gavin Friday's **Ich Liebe Dich,** to the music of Kurt Weill, at the Dublin Theatre Festival 2001. He was Production Director with **Riverdance: The Show,** for two years, travelling world-wide to oversee the three Riverdance companies and special events, and was Artistic Director of Operating Theatre (with Roger Doyle) from 1984-1989. During this period he also collaborated with James Coleman as lighting designer on **Ignotum per Ignotius,** at the Douglas Hyde Gallery, and as lighting and video designer on the installation/performance **Guaire: an Allegory** in Dunguaire, Kinvara.

John recently directed **Hit and Run,** Ireland's first dance film, which won the main prizes at the Toronto Moving Pictures and New York Dance On Screen festivals. He has also directed and produced documentaries on the Dingle Wrens' Day and the Berlin years of Agnes Bernelle. He was a director with RTE for 12 years, during which time he directed hundreds of television programmes and created the visual style of numerous TV series including **Nighthawks, The Blackbird and The Bell** and **PopScene.** In 1995, he directed the **Eurovision Song Contest.**

PAMELA McQUEEN STAGE MANAGER

Pamela has previously worked with Rough Magic as Stage Manager on **Copenhagen, Midden** and **Dead Funny**. She was Production Manager for **Why I Hate the Circus, Describe Joe, Much Ado About Nothing, The Good Thief** and **Rum & Vodka** for Greenlight Productions, of which she is a founder member. Other production management includes the Dublin Fringe Festivals in 1999 and 2000; **Miss Canary Islands** and **Dead Boys** for Focus Theatre, and stage management includes **When I Was God** (Everyman Palace) and **Sons and Daughters, Lolita, On Such As We** and **Down The Line** (Peacock). Pamela also acted as Producer for the Greenlight/Project Summer School of Theatre Design 2001.

KATHY STRACHAN COSTUME DESIGNER

Kathy trained at the Central School Of Art And Design, London. Rough Magic productions include **Dead Funny, Halloween Night, New Morning, Hidden Charges** and **Three Days Of Rain**.

Other theatre includes **Sive** (Druid); **Twenty Grand** and **In A Little World of Our Own** (both Peacock); **The White Devil** (Den Nationale Scene, Bergen, Norway); **Rainsnakes** (Young Vic Studio); **Playboy of the Western World** and **The Silver Tassie** (both Almeida) and **Dengang N å** (Rogaland Theatre Stavanger, Norway).

Television and film credits as Costume Designer include **Bachelors Walk, On The Nose, Saltwater, The Closer You Get, I Went Down** and **Vicious Circle**.

PAULA TIERNEY STAGE DIRECTOR

Paula's previous Rough Magic productions include **Copenhagen, Pentecost, Northern Star, Danti Dan, Hidden Charges, The Dogs** and **Digging for Fire**.

Paula is a graduate of UCC and has spent ten years as a stage manager/operator, on productions for Fishamble, Second Age, Bickerstaffe, Barabbas, Galloglass, Calypso, Red Kettle, the Everyman Cork, the Gate Theatre and the Peacock. She has toured nationally and internationally with Opera Theatre Company, including **Zaide** (Antwerp and Belgian tour), **The Magic Flute, Cosi Fan Tutte, The Marriage of Figaro, La Vera Constanza,** and **Amadigi** (Melbourne Festival, BAM New York, Lisbon, Porto and Paris). She has been Stage Director for both the Covent Garden and Buxton opera festivals and at home for Opera Ireland on **Die Fledermaus, La Traviata, Boris Gudunov** and **Aïda.** Other recent productions include **Macbeth** (Second Age); **Siberia** and **Orleanskaya Deva** (Wexford Festival Opera); **Rent** and **Mother Courage** (Olympia); **The Quest of the Good People** (Pavilion, Dun Laoghaire) and **Kvetch** (Kilkenny Arts Festival).

Cover image: Shiver by Rebecca McLynn, print, oil, wax, ink, acrylic medium and sand on canvas, 2002, used by kind permission of the artist.

Further information on Rebecca McLynn is available from: Sarah Myerscough Fine Art, 15-16 Brooks Mews, London W1, + 44 20 7495 0069, www.sarahmyerscough.com, or by contacting the artist direct at rebecca_longley@hotmail.com.

ROUGH MAGIC PRODUCTIONS

2002
SCAN (international play-readings)

COPENHAGEN by Michael Frayn - IP

2001
MIDDEN by Morna Regan - WP

PLAYS⁴ (international play-readings)

DEAD FUNNY by Terry Johnson - IP

2000
THREE DAYS OF RAIN
by Richard Greenberg - IP

PLAYS⁴ (international play-readings)

PENTECOST by Stewart Parker - USP

1999
THE WHISPERERS - WP

BOOMTOWN by Pom Boyd, Declan Hughes
and Arthur Riordan - WP

1998
THE SCHOOL FOR SCANDAL
by Richard Brinsley Sheridan

1997
HALLOWE'EN NIGHT by Declan Hughes - WP

MRS. SWEENEY by Paula Meehan - WP

1996
PENTECOST by Stewart Parker

NORTHERN STAR by Stewart Parker

1995
DANTI-DAN by Gina Moxley - WP

PENTECOST by Stewart Parker

1994
LADY WINDERMERE'S FAN by Oscar Wilde

HIDDEN CHARGES by Arthur Riordan - WP

DOWN ONTO BLUE by Pom Boyd - WP

1993
NEW MORNING by Declan Hughes - WP

THE WAY OF THE WORLD
by William Congreve

1992
DIGGING FOR FIRE by Declan Hughes - UKP

THE DOGS by Donal O'Kelly - WP

BAT THE FATHER RABBIT THE SON
by Donal O'Kelly

THE EMERGENCY SESSION
by Arthur Riordan - WP

LOVE AND A BOTTLE by George Farquhar,
adapted by Declan Hughes

1991
LOVE AND A BOTTLE by George Farquhar,
adapted by Declan Hughes - WP

I CAN'T GET STARTED
by Declan Hughes - USP

LADY WINDERMERE'S FAN by Oscar Wilde

DIGGING FOR FIRE by Declan Hughes - WP

1990

LADY WINDERMERE'S FAN by Oscar Wilde
I CAN'T GET STARTED
by Declan Hughes · WP

BAT THE FATHER RABBIT THE SON
by Donal O'Kelly

1989

BAT THE FATHER RABBIT THE SON
by Donal O'Kelly · UKP
A HANDFUL OF STARS by Billy Roche · IP

SPOKESONG by Stewart Parker
OUR COUNTRY'S GOOD
by Timberlake Wertenbaker · IP

1988

THE WHITE DEVIL by John Webster · IP
TOM AND VIV by Michael Hastings · IP
TEA AND SEA AND SHAKESPEARE
a new version by Thomas Kilroy

BAT THE FATHER RABBIT THE SON
by Donal O'Kelly · WP
SERIOUS MONEY by Caryl Churchill · IP

1987

NIGHTSHADE by Stewart Parker
ROAD by Jim Cartwright · IP
THE TEMPEST by Shakespeare
THE SILVER TASSIE by Sean O'Casey

A MUG'S GAME adaptation by the
company of Le Bourgeois Gentilhomme
and Everyman · IP

1986

MIDNITE AT THE STARLITE
by Michael Hastings
CAUCASIAN CHALK CIRCLE
by Bertolt Brecht
BETRAYAL by Harold Pinter · IP
DOGG'S HAMLET, CAHOOT'S
MACBETH by Tom Stoppard

DECADENCE by Steven Berkoff
AUNT DAN AND LEMON
by Wallace Shawn · IP
BLOODY POETRY by Howard Brenton
THE COUNTRY WIFE by William Wycherly
THE WOMAN IN WHITE adapted by Declan
Hughes from Wilkie Collins's novel · IP

1985

TOP GIRLS by Caryl Churchill
SEXUAL PERVERSITY IN CHICAGO
by David Mamet
VICTORY by Howard Barker · IP
NO END OF BLAME by Howard Barker · IP

THE ONLY JEALOUSY OF EMER by WB Yeats
MIDNITE AT THE STARLITE
by Michael Hastings · IP
CAUCASIAN CHALK CIRCLE
by Bertolt Brecht

1984

TALBOT'S BOX by Thomas Kilroy
FANSHEN by David Hare · IP
THE BIG HOUSE by Brendan Behan
THIRST by Myles na gCopaleen
DECADENCE by Steven Berkoff · IP

SEXUAL PERVERSITY IN CHICAGO
by David Mamet
TOP GIRLS by Caryl Churchill · IP
AMERICAN BUFFALO by David Mamet

WP = World première
IP = Irish première

UKP = UK première
USP = American première

FOR ROUGH MAGIC

Shiver

.

To Isobel and Heather

Shiver premiered at the Project Arts Centre, Dublin, on
28 March 2003. The cast was as follows:

Richard   Peter Hanly
Jenny   Cathy White
Marion   Cathy Belton
Kevin   Paul Hickey

Director Lynne Parker
Set and Lighting Designer John Comiskey
Sound Designer Cormac Carroll

Characters

Richard, *forty*
Jenny, *thirty-seven*
Marion, *forty*
Kevin, *thirty-eight*

Act One

Music: 'The Folks Who Live on the Hill' – Jo Stafford.

Enter **Richard O'Grady**, *forty and* **Jennifer Ryan**, *thirty-seven. They talk to us.*

Richard   So, home we came at last . . .

Jenny   'Home we came?' You sure about that, Richard?

Richard   I think so. Well, we came home, didn't we?

Jenny   Oh, I know we came home. It's just, 'Home we came?'

Richard   Gives it a little lift. You don't like it?

Jenny   I don't not like it, it's just . . . you decide.

Richard (*short pause*)   So, home we came at last, after many years of wandering –

Jenny   Just, we don't want it to sound too . . . mythic, do we?

Richard   Don't we?

Jenny   You know, as if we'd been 'In Exile'. We were only in the States, after all.

Richard   You think it sounds a bit grand?

Jenny   That would be the danger.

Richard   We should just . . . tell it like it was.

Jenny   Insofar as that's possible.

Richard   All right. No myth, no exile. Home. (*Short pause.*) We live in a new granite house –

Jenny   No, explain a *bit* about the past, *why* we came back.

Richard   We didn't care about the past in those days, remember?

Jenny   Even so, you need a little history.

Richard   History was finished, Jenny. History was over. (*To us.*) We live in a new granite house at the base of an old quarry. There are four other houses.

Jenny   Two are occupied by visiting executives. These change every six months or so, but effectively they're identical, they exude an executive spoor, neither male nor female but executron, they set off before dawn, they return after dusk, they don't really need houses, a shelf would do them. An executron hutch.

Richard   We all have to work hard these days. That's just the way it is.

Jenny   Then there's the Pattersons. They're retired. Mr Patterson wears a collar and tie every day, and is always zipping off to play golf. Mrs Patterson dyes her hair jet black and is very cross indeed. What goes on there?

Richard   They're just an ordinary couple, I don't know why you have to turn them into such a big deal.

Jenny   An ordinary couple. What happened to them? Once they were happy, suddenly they never would be again, The End.

Richard   And then there's Marion and Kevin.

Enter **Kevin McBride**, *thirty-eight, and* **Marion Johnson**, *forty, with wine and flowers.*

Jenny   And Baby Thomas.

Kevin *plugs a baby monitor into a wall socket.*

Richard   Marion's a graphic designer. She heads up the creative team at Ferguson Gough.

Jenny   Marion, in fact, is a bit of an executron.

Richard   And Kevin is on leave. He's a teacher –

Jenny   A Poet.

Richard   An unpublished poet.

Jenny   He had a poem in *The Times*.

Richard   Over a year ago.

Jenny   Every writer is unpublished until he's not.

Richard   That's true. 'Until.'

Jenny   You wouldn't know anyway. Poetry.

Richard   That's true too. I wouldn't have a clue. For now, Kevin minds Baby Thomas.

Jenny   And Baby Thomas . . . is the baby!

Over the monitor, the baby gurgles.

Marion *and* **Kevin** *talk to us.*

Marion   Richard and Jenny. We were thrilled when they moved in.

Kevin   They were our new best friends. And we needed friends.

Marion   A couple our own age, at last. Their energy was simply awesome. They had that whole American can-do thing.

Kevin   It was a little daunting.

Marion   It was inspirational: the creativity, the ambition, the vision. They were the latest wave.

Kevin   Hard to avoid being swept away.

Marion   They were our new best friends.

Kevin   It doesn't end well.

The baby gurgles.

Jenny   Aw, the little baba.

Richard   What's the range on that thing?

Kevin   Dunno. Think it would carry across to the Pattersons?

Marion   You're becoming obsessed.

Kevin   Mary and me. You wouldn't understand.

Marion   It's not a sex thing –

Kevin   It's a cake thing.

Marion   She drops buns in. Puddings. Flans. Pastries.

Jenny   She barely says hello to me.

Richard   Or me. Maybe it's Baby Thomas.

Kevin   She's not interested in the baby. She has her own grandchildren. I'm telling you, we're having an affair, conducted exclusively through cake. She comes up the drive with a strawberry cream sponge – won't come past the porch – then later, I return the plate and thank her, and she blushes and shuts her door. We've barely exchanged a dozen words. But I've put on half a stone in a month.

Marion   You could always not eat them.

Kevin   I couldn't betray Mary like that.

Marion   It's not a cake thing, it's a Mammy thing.

Kevin   You're almost certainly correct.

Jenny   All Irishmen want to marry their mothers.

Marion   All Irishmen are already married to their mothers. An Irish wife is the other woman. Oh God! Richard, I'm sorry!

Richard   It's all right. (*To us.*) My mother is dying. (*To* **Marion**.) Don't be silly.

Jenny (*to us*)   She's been dying for years.

Richard   She'll outlive us all.

Jenny (*to us*) I wouldn't put it past her. (*To* **Kevin**.) Richard's mother used to look like Lana Turner.

Richard   She looked like Jo Stafford.

Jenny   I thought she *sang* like Jo Stafford.

Richard   That as well. She was Ireland's answer to Jo Stafford.

Jenny   Why does Ireland always have to have an answer to everything?

Richard   Where's this wine from, Kevin, Argentina?

Kevin   Uruguay.

Jenny   Apparently they're the coming nation. In wine terms.

Marion   I read that somewhere.

Richard   It's hard to keep up.

Marion   It's impossible. Everything's changing so quickly. But sure, who am I telling? You're the ones with the dot.com!

Jenny (*to us*)   Oh My God How Embarrassing! I am *so* sorry. 'Dot.com', honestly. It's like 'Boutique' or 'Fondue Set', it already sounds so dated.

Richard   Sorry.

Jenny   I told you, Richard, history!

Richard   We came home at last –

Jenny   Just before things went totally mental, property-wise –

Richard   To establish our own –

Jenny   Cringe if you must –

Richard/Jenny   Dot.com start-up!

Later. **Richard** *and* **Jenny** *talk to* **Marion** *and* **Kevin**.

Richard   I'd been working in financial services: first in New York, then in Houston and Atlanta.

Jenny   Once, nobody knew what financial services meant. Now we all know it means How To Pay Less Tax!

Richard   There's a lot more to it than that.

Jenny   Absolutely, for all your blue-chip clients like J.J. MacTaggert, where it meant: How To Pay No Tax At All!

Richard   I never did anything illegal. But it was a pretty depressing way of making a living. Most of my clients were –

Jenny   Smug corporate Caesars. Bloated white plutocrats.

Richard   Just a little *too* rich. I'm not one for high taxes, but some of these guys were worth tens of millions, and all they thought about was the government 'stealing' their money. It made you feel –

Jenny   Like lining them up against a wall and –

Richard   Just a little queasy.
And then we met.

Marion   I love hearing how couples met. How the central event in your life is so completely random. How we're all at the mercy of chance.

Kevin   Or Fate.

Marion   Whatever.

Kevin   There is a difference –

Jenny   I was waitressing, as usual –

Richard   You had a business supplying gourmet lunches to deskbound executrons like me.

Jenny   Yeah. I was waitressing, as usual –

Richard   You were running a catering company.

Jenny   Into the ground.

Richard   It would've come good, it just needed time.

Jenny   My best customer. Three lunches a day.

Richard   It wasn't a food thing.

Jenny   And significantly, my best customer wasn't interested in the food.

Marion   The service is just as important.

Richard   Service is the most important thing. Service has replaced manufacturing as the Number One Industry today. It's just not cool to make things any more!

Marion   So you met.

Jenny   And we married.

Richard   And Jenny – I mean, it was all Jenny's idea –

Jenny   Excuse me, you proposed.

Richard   Not the marriage, the business. The website.

Jenny   You wanted to work for yourself.

Richard   But I'd never've taken the plunge on my own.

Jenny   Richard had savings. He actually earned more money than he spent. I'd never woken up with anyone like that before.

Richard   Enough for the deposit on the old house anyway. And seed money for the business.

Jenny   And that's the story of us. We didn't like our jobs, so we decided to make up new ones.

Richard   Take a chance on the future.

Marion   What else is there? Right, Kevin?

Kevin   Sorry, what?

Marion   Kevin was in a dream.

Jenny   Kevin was bored stupid.

Kevin   Not at all. What?

Marion   Kevin doesn't do business.

Jenny   Kevin's right. Business is not as fascinating as certain people – funnily enough, almost always business people – think.

Kevin   I don't know –

Jenny   Used to be, business people were content with having all the money and all the power. But now they want to be loved as well. Fuck them.

Richard   We are business people.

Jenny   I know. Fuck us and all.

Kevin   Self-hatred. The white man's burden.

Jenny   White woman, Kevin. White men can't hate that hard.

Kevin   Can we not?

Jenny   Well. I suppose you can *try*.

Pause.

Richard   Kevin. How's the poetry coming?

Kevin *talks to us.*

Kevin   Let's be clear – I am not a poet. I wrote one poem, and my then-girlfriend-now-wife submitted it to *The Times*, and they printed it, and ever since – I mean, it's hard enough being a poet if you are one, it's bloody annoying people thinking you're a poet when you're not. It's like that joke, the punchline to which goes: you shag one sheep – you write one poem . . .

I read somewhere that poets on average earn eighty-four pence a year directly from poetry. Well, that's if you don't let Seamus Heaney into the sample. Add Famous Seamus and everyone ends up with three grand. I quote from memory.

Anyway, I am not a poet. Only, when I deny it, people think
it's false modesty and arrogance. It's fucking ridiculous,
actually. But it's become too boring to explain it all the time
so:

Slow but steady, Richard, slow but steady.

Richard   Only we were wondering . . . Jenny was
wondering –

Jenny   If you had any new material, you might like us to
post it on the site. I mean, we'd pay you, of course, and you
could retain all the rights to it – if you had any new
material, that is, even in progress – no pressure though.

Marion   I think that's a brilliant idea, Kevin. Get some of
the new material out there.

Kevin (*to us*)   'The new material.'

Richard   No pressure though.

Jenny   We've got some really exciting projects lined up for
the launch issue.

Marion   Have you come up with a name yet?

Jenny   Richard.

Richard   51st State.

Marion   51st State?

Richard   51st State!

Richard *and* **Jenny** *talk to us.*

Jenny   I goaded him into it, I concede that; I harried and
jostled, I wounded him into change. But he took to it, my
conservative husband, he embraced the new with a
convert's fervour. So much so that there were times when I
thought Richard has lost his mind. Richard is now almost
completely insane.

Richard   The luminiferous ether of cyberspace! A
constellation of electronic hosts scattered about the Net, like

stars hung high in the heavenly firmament! A Zodiac of Infinite Freedom and Opportunity!

Kevin   51st State? Of America, like?

Jenny   What do you think?

Marion   It's perfect.

Richard   It was Jenny's idea.

Jenny   It's hardly original. But it captures what's going on now. The whole global thing.

Marion   Absolutely. Everywhere there are new markets, companies using the new technology, America's at the root of it –

Richard (*a surge*)   The Internet is way more democratic than any country could be. And 51st State will be at the heart of that new democracy, bypassing governments, empowering the real rulers: the people.

Jenny (*caught up in it*)   51st State is about letting go the past and reinventing yourself: it's off with the old, the green fields, the simple faith, the diddly-eye, goodbye!

Richard   51st State is about the future. About the day after tomorrow!

There's a silence, which it somehow falls to **Kevin** *to fill.*

Kevin   Wow.

Richard (*to us*)   And then we asked them what their news was.

Jenny (*to us*)   As if you couldn't guess – she was showing already.

Kevin   On you go then, Marion.

Marion   No, you tell them.

Kevin (*to us*)   So I told Jenny and Richard that Marion was pregnant again, and of course they were delighted and congratulated us and hugged her and made a big fuss, but I noticed Marion looked a little subdued. And I remembered that we had two items of news. So while they were opening the champagne, I told them the other thing: that US conglomerate NPK had bought out Ferguson Gough, and Marion and three other heads of department had been given salary increases and shares in the company.

Back to **Jenny** *and* **Richard**.

Kevin   Sorry, I got it the wrong way round, I thought we should have the best news first, I know the other's a bit of an anti-climax after hearing about the second baby.

Marion   Yes. It will, however anti-climactically, ensure that we're able to *afford* the second baby.

A not altogether happy pause. **Kevin** *pretends he hasn't heard this;* **Marion** *pretends she hasn't said it.*

They all have full champagne glasses.

Richard   A toast then? To new life, and new work –

Jenny   To babies and shares –

Kevin   To 51st State –

Marion   To the day after tomorrow!

That's the one.

All   The Day After Tomorrow!

Kevin *and* **Marion**.

Kevin   Everything used to be fine. Marion'd see Thomas in the morning before she left for work and usually make it home in time to tuck him in and I'd cook dinner and that would be our day. Not the most dramatic life, but who needs drama? And then Richard and Jenny moved in and started up 51st State, and suddenly it was no longer enough, in the eyes of my wife, no longer legal, it seemed, under the laws of the New Economy, for a man to spend his days looking after his eighteen-month-old son.

Marion *is getting ready for work.* **Kevin** *is writing.*

Marion   You're up early.

Kevin   Couldn't sleep.

Marion   Are you writing?

Kevin   I am.

Marion   Oh, Kevin! Have you finished? Read me what you've got.

Kevin   Pasta. Green veg. Booze. Tins of tomatoes. Mouthwash. Nappies. Baby wipes. Coriander.

Marion   Very funny.

Kevin   We need groceries.

Marion   Can't you get them? I've kind of a busy day lined up.

Kevin   They've stopped delivering.

Marion   Well, can't you learn to drive, and then get them?

Kevin   Can we wait that long for nappies?

Marion *takes the list.*

Marion   What size nappies?

Kevin   Four.

Marion   And what brand?

Kevin   Whatever.

Marion   Because last time I got the wrong ones.

Kevin   Well, they were fine, as it happened. Get them again.

Marion   Why couldn't you sleep?

Kevin   Coffee late at night.

Marion   You need to do more.

Kevin   I'm with Thomas all the time, that's kind of a busy day in itself.

Marion   You know I didn't mean that.

Kevin   What more do I need to do then?

Marion   Get those new poems together for Richard and Jenny. God, 51st State sounds so exciting, doesn't it?

Kevin   No.

Pause.

Marion   Or why not write a column about being a stay-at-home dad? You know my friend Aimee's an editor at *The Times* now –

Kevin   Marion, I drank too much coffee. I'm perfectly OK. I don't want to write anything.

Marion   You need to do *something*.

Kevin   I do do 'something'.

Marion   We can afford a crèche, Kevin.

Kevin   I could go back to work, I suppose.

Marion   I don't mean teach, I mean – something creative. You're a creative person.

Kevin   No I'm not.

Marion   I'll call Aimee, I'm sure she'll want to talk to you.

Kevin   About what, my shopping lists? I can do her one a week.

Marion   You're impossible. Give Thomas a kiss from me. Oh, and Kevin, the washing, please. A machine-load a day, that's all it takes.

Exit **Marion**.

Kevin   I mean, it was a deal we had made: Marion earned more than I did, and loved her job, and we agreed that one of us should look after Baby Thomas, and I was happy to be the one, and she was happy too. And Mrs Patterson said: 'Aren't you great the way you go round with the baba like that? In my day now the men wouldn't've been caught dead.' And she gave me a loaf of banana bread.

But the point was, I liked it. I liked taking Thomas on walks to the ruined church at the top of the old granite quarry. I liked his sweet-sour, musky, milky smell, and his dark, grave eyes, and his hot little body, and his laugh. His laughter from another room, or when he had just roused himself, and was laughing for reasons he couldn't or wouldn't share with me, or maybe just laughing with the sheer joy of being awake, and how often do you hear that?

Richard *and* **Jenny**.

Richard *is wearing combat trousers and a short-sleeved shirt.*

Richard   I'm seeing Andy at eleven.

Jenny   Andy the Programmer.

Richard   No, Andy the Web Designer. Peter's the programmer. I'm meeting Peter for lunch.

Jenny   And you've got a rough budget.

Richard   I've got a yes-or-no budget. But they're both starting out too. So it's in their interest –

Jenny   We'll be on their résumés.

Richard   So it's in their interest to get the site up.

Jenny   Shirt out.

Richard   Sorry. (*He lets his shirt-tails hang out.*) Then I've to run the financial projections past Michael.

Jenny   He's seen the business plan? And Gerry?

Richard   Everyone's seen the business plan. Everyone loves the business plan.

Jenny   Everyone loves it? Do they?

Richard   Yes.

Jenny   Richard?

Richard   They love it, yeah, they love – the *idea* of it.

Jenny   But the practicalities: the customer base, gap in the market, the . . . so on. Michael recognised the potential? Michael liked that, did he?

Richard   The idea of it. The whole idea of 51st State. Everybody loves the idea. And the business plan – which you wrote – which you *devised* – is a – a visionary document. Which contains – which *conveys* – the idea of 51st State. And since all it is, at the moment, is an idea, that's all they have to go on. And believe me, they love it.

Jenny   Better than if they hate it.

Richard   Well, that's what I thought. And then I'm meeting Gerry in the Horseshoe. He's got a couple of guys who might want to invest.

Jenny   When did that come up?

Richard   Last night, he called. They're just, I don't know, clients of his, guys he goes to the races with. Camel-hair men.

Jenny   Shouldn't I come? I mean, are you going to be pitching –

Richard   No, it's just a drink, not a formal – I mean, these guys are loaded, but they barely know what the Internet is, let alone – it's a softly-softly thing.

Jenny   A new dress. And I can flirt. And laugh at their 'jokes'.

Richard   Sure. Actually, why don't you do it and I'll come home. Those sort of guys always think I'm some kind of –

Jenny   They won't if I'm there.

Richard (*smiles*)   No, they won't, will they? Horseshoe at six then.

He has his laptop bag, and a backpack. His shirt-tails hang below his soft zip jacket. He wears heavy black shoes.

So: do I look the very model of an IT entrepreneur?

Jenny   Not in those shoes. Trainers, Richard.

Richard   Trainers. OK.

Richard *changes his shoes, puts on his trainers.*

Jenny   I'm calling the writers. And the photographers.

Richard   You've got a list.

Jenny   I've got a list. A Contributors Long List.

Richard   Who's on it?

Jenny   Would it mean anything if I told you?

Richard   No.

Jenny   Well then. You look great.

Richard   I look unemployed.

Jenny   Richard!

Richard   I'm a suit, Jenny. Deep down, I'm a suit.

Jenny   No you're not. No you're not.

Richard   No I'm not.

Jenny   Not any more. Say it. I am –

Richard   I am not a suit.

Jenny   Good.

Richard   I am not a suit! I am a free man!

Jenny   That's the way. Don't let the bigger boys steal your lunch.

Richard (*clenched fist*)   51st State!

Jenny   You bet!

Exit **Richard**.

Jenny   He was a suit though, to the depth of his soul, like one of those men you see at the weekends, dressed in casual clothes their wives have bought for them, pushing buggies or eating ice creams or buying cinema tickets, looking like impostors, undercover executrons, Men Not Wearing Suits.

Richard   I wanted to explain to people in the street: I'm at work, actually, I'm going to a meeting. This is what the go-getters are wearing these days! This is the New Economy on the March!

Jenny   Andy the Web Designer and Peter the Programmer both agreed to work on a deferred fee basis. And Michael the Accountant and Gerry the Solicitor are Richard's oldest friends, so they can wait.

Richard   Michael admitted he was no dot.com expert, but he acknowledged that tech stocks were flying high, said there was plenty of venture capital out there waiting to be invested.

Jenny   We were never going public, that wasn't the plan – although we talked about it, in those first few carried-away days.

Richard   51st State heads for its IPO, 51st State launches at fifty mil., 51st State finishes the day at three hundred million!

Jenny   Tech shares, millionaires!

Richard   They were insane times back then. A lot of money was being invested in ideas that were, frankly, ridiculous – the dot.com MO seemed to be, spend as much money as possible marketing the business, and don't worry about profits, they'll come later.

Jenny   I sometimes think if we had gone to the States, got an investment bank behind us, Morgan Stanley or Goldman Sachs, done the whole investment roadshow, we could easily have floated for forty or fifty dollars a share. And if there were a million shares . . .

Richard   But then you're tied in, you can't turn around and start selling your own shares in the company if you're the CEO, it tends to undermine the market's confidence just a shade.

Jenny   So if our share price dropped, we'd have had to hang in there while everyone else bailed.

Richard   Which is why we decided to keep it small.

Jenny   Although sometimes, if your projections are too conservative, people think you lack the confidence, the drive to succeed.

Richard   We did end up pitching to Gerry's friends at the Horseshoe – but I don't think we were ready for it.

Jenny   It was Gerry's friends who weren't ready. Camel-hair Neanderthals.

Richard   Heavy hitters in the markets, a lot smarter than they looked. And they were open to ideas. But – well – maybe we just – I don't know, weren't in sync that day.

Jenny   It was not our problem, it was their problem, we were trying to sell 51st State, you shouldn't have had to justify the whole idea of e-business to them.

Richard   Maybe we were underprepared. The synergy between us –

Jenny   Cavemen with cigars, Richard. It was not our problem, it was their problem.

Richard   Although our inability to attract investors soon became our problem.

Kevin *and* **Marion**.

Kevin   The houses were built with granite from the quarry. First time it had been drilled in a hundred years.

Marion   They're not solid granite. Just an outer shell.

Kevin   But a living connection: to the quarry, the ruined church, the living rock. Hard to dream the future, in a place so ancient and grave.

Marion   The ruined church. He became obsessed. I can't stand the sight of it now.

Kevin   Look the other way then. Look in the Pattersons' window. Watch them dance.

Marion   On Saturday nights, Mr and Mrs Patterson dress up, and play the old tunes, and dance together in their living room.

Kevin   They're still good dancers.

Pause.

Marion   We bought the house off the plans. Four bedrooms. More than we needed, and more expensive than we thought we could afford, but that was '95, and they've rocketed since then.

Kevin   I'd been teaching for fifteen years, so I had the bones of a deposit salted away.

Marion   And I'd just got a new job. Creative Director of a Graphic Design Consultancy. On a salary of . . . of a hell of a lot more than I'd ever had before.

Kevin   A lot, lot more than me. So let's just –

Kevin/Marion   Buy a house!

Marion   It was open-plan, big plate-glass windows, sprawling garden . . .

Kevin   The kind of house they weren't supposed to build any more.

Marion   Tall and tan and young and lovely, tennis games and swimming parties and barbecues.

Kevin   Doris Day and Rock Hudson. Although . . . not literally Rock Hudson. Or Doris Day, for that matter.

Marion   Like our parents might have done it, if they'd grown up in a kind of fantasy movie version of the American 1950s. And feeling at last like it was OK to do it like your parents might have. Only with extra sex.

Kevin   Or, after Baby Thomas came, *without* extra sex. And how do you know how much sex our parents had anyway? Why would you want to know, Jesus.

Marion   See, I had this picture in my head – my dad, tall and tan in his swimming trunks, the green grass of our big back garden rippling beneath a summer blue sky – the garden couldn't have been that big, it was just a suburban semi-d, but in my memory it's vast, like a meadow. Daddy all crinkle-eyed smiles, so handsome, and Mum in a summer frock, pale green with yellow roses on it – roses or sunflowers – is it too much to want that back? Is it too much to want, if not to do better than your parents did, then at least to do as well?

Jenny at her laptop.

Jenny   The deal was: I'd be the artistic one – dreamy and wild, fey and intuitive, transported for days by some grand, impractical vagary. He'd be the rock. But then everything got a little topsy-turvy. I'd be here, trying to organise the content – or simply provide some – when –

*Enter **Richard**, with laptop and backpack.*

Richard   Every morning, on desktops all over the world, Korea to Kansas City, 51st State will tell it like it is! We are the microcosm, the behavioural laboratory for the future!

Jenny   What did Michael say to that?

Richard   He said it was the most incredibly brilliant idea he'd ever heard!

Jenny   No, that's what you said; what did he say?

Richard   He said it would be a long time before we'd see any money from it.

Jenny   Well, you knew that, didn't you?

Richard   Of course! Michael's thinking like I used to, like a number-cruncher, that's all he can see now, the bottom line. What he's missing is the bigger picture: 51st State on every computer screen in the world, like a universal TV channel! Set out your stall for the entire world market: that's the kind of exposure advertisers are going to pay big money for.

Jenny   What did he say to that?

Richard   He said we'd need something major to get on every computer screen in the world. He actually suggested –

Jenny   Yes?

Richard   Well, asked, if we thought we could get something from Seamus Heaney. So I said I'd have to check with you.

Jenny   Something from Seamus Heaney.

Richard   Yes. A new poem. I suppose. Or . . . whatever. He is poetry, isn't he, Seamus Heaney?

Jenny   Seamus Heaney? Hello? Because Seamus Heaney is so *not* what 51st State is about, Richard.

Richard   I thought that.

Jenny   I mean, new paradigms and cutting edges and the future and so on, this is not Seamus Heaney.

Richard   I told him that. But he said – and maybe it's not entirely a bad point – that you could hook people in with

Heaney, and then persuade them to stick around for the other stuff.

Jenny   Richard, 51st State *is* the other stuff.

Richard   He did win the Nobel Prize, Jenny.

Jenny   So did Yeats and Beckett, will we stick them in too? This is not a Celtic souvenir shop.

Richard   I know.

Jenny   It's not some Irish theme pub on the tour-bus circuit.

Richard   You're right.

Jenny   I mean, you know what we're doing here.

Richard   You're absolutely right. Forget it.

Jenny   OK?

Richard   OK. Good. I've got a meeting with Andy. He's got some mock-ups of the site ready. I'd better go. (*He lingers.*) Excellent! 51st State!

Exit **Richard**.

Marion *and* **Kevin**.

Marion   Aimee, the features editor from *The Times*, came out specially one evening to meet Kevin. As a favour to me.

Kevin   We had a drink in the Corner House, the oldest pub in the village. Mineral water, pint.

Marion   Aimee had quite a budget back then: more ads than they could print, more pages than they could fill. Crying out for contributors, in those boom days.

Kevin   She was very impressive, absolutely; you don't get to do a job like that by accident. Very sharp, very *groomed*.

Marion   Aimee tends to get what she wants.

Kevin I just wasn't interested in giving it to her. Diary of an apparently hapless but secretly expert stay-at-home dad, with his nappy know-how and his delectable dinners and his winsome one-liners. A shambling domestic pet of a man.

Marion Kevin said he'd write about the ruined church instead. About a gold rush, and some religious apparition that occurred in the quarry a hundred years ago. And Aimee said not for her he wouldn't.

Kevin So everyone's happy. Except for Marion.

Marion I didn't marry you so that you could be my wife.

Kevin I'm ready to ride you whenever you want. Would your wife say that?

Marion I'm serious.

Kevin Yes, you are, aren't you, trying to bounce me into doing a job I have no wish to do, for money we don't need. Why are you doing that?

Marion Because you're losing the thing, the inner thing you had, the spark, the drive, the edge.

Kevin And writing a column about minding a two-year-old would be edgy, would it?

Marion You could have suggested an alternative.

Kevin I did.

Marion An acceptable alternative.

Kevin Marion, here's the thing: all writers, good, bad or indifferent, prose, poetry or some unhappy mixture, sooner or later, they all have to sit on their own and actually, physically, you know, write. Now have you ever seen me doing that?

Marion When Thomas was born.

Kevin When our son was born, yes, I wrote a poem, singular. I'd bet there are thousands of non-writers who can roll out a poem for the big family events, laureates of the hatch, match and dispatch school of verse. Why do you –

Marion   All right then, write about this gold rush then, or religious apparitions or whatever the fuck it is, just do something before I –

Kevin   Before you *what?*

Pause.

Marion   I'm tired now, I'm going to bed.

She doesn't move.

Kevin (*to us*)   How did it happen? That you're continually having the same argument, and it feels like it's always been like this? Because it hasn't always been like this, it really hasn't.

Pause.

Marion   I used to work for a design co-op called 'Better Ways'. We did posters for independent theatre shows, and logos for small non-profit organisations, and flyers for benefit nights and protest marches, and obviously we didn't make much money, but we did all right, and anyway, in your twenties, you're not that bothered about money; at least, we weren't. But then, same old story, you get older, you get married, you're ready to sell out. And there's nothing worse than being ready to sell out and nobody asking. Makes you very sour. So when FGC offered me three times what I'd make in a year, it simply never occurred to me to refuse it. And the Better Ways girls understood, although they did seem to find it incredibly hilarious that FGC – Ferguson Gough Consultancy – could also stand for Fat Greedy Cow. But if you're forty and you're still living like you're in your twenties, there's just something wrong, I don't care who you are.

Kevin   After the takeover, NPK moved Ferguson Gough to a business park out in west Dublin somewhere, so Marion leaves at six thirty each morning, before Thomas wakes, and she never gets home now before nine, well after he's gone to bed. So the weekends are her time to catch up. It's hard for her, and then Thomas is always a bit nervy at first and makes strange noises and clings to me and cries, and Marion's wrecked from the working week anyway, so the whole thing can be a bit tense. And then she cries and says, 'I don't know who I am any more,' so I take Thomas out for a walk, and when I get back she's asleep. And there are work calls all through the weekend now, and she's always got stuff to prepare for Monday morning. And then she'll say, 'This place is a pigsty,' and spend three hours hoovering. And I might brighten matters up by saying something like, 'We never seem to have any time for us any more,' or 'Why can't things be like they used to be?' or 'I'm sorry I ever married you.' Of course, I never actually say, 'I'm sorry I ever married you.' I just say, 'I'm sorry.' All the time.

Marion   I wish Kevin would stop saying sorry all the time. I wish I had some time – any time – for myself. I wish I could sleep for a year.

Kevin   I don't know what I wish any more.

Marion   The Better Ways girls didn't understand, actually. They said, 'You're a fat greedy cow.' Kevin said, 'If they were the best friends you had, fuck them.' I never see them now. I never see anyone from before.

Kevin   Though we were happier then.

Marion   Deep down though, I think Kevin agreed with them. I think he really thought I had sold out.

Kevin   Back when we didn't have a standard of living, we somehow seemed to have more of a life.

Marion   I just don't have time to dwell on it, Kevin, I'm tired and I'm going to bed.

Kevin   And just as well she did, because forcing your heavily pregnant wife to admit she despises you is not as much fun as it sounds.

Marion   I don't 'despise' him. I just find his endlessly complacent self-satisfied domestic blissfulness very irritating. And not altogether convincing. And I still end up doing all the washing, and cleaning, and . . . sorry, it's . . . it's nothing personal. It's strictly marriage.

Richard *and* **Jenny**.

Jenny   And then Richard would swing back into bottom-line mode, which, in contrast to his cyber-evangelism, was almost reassuring.

Richard   Jen, this is looney-tune stuff.

Jenny   What is?

Richard   The rates of pay. Michael says we're offering contributors twice the going rate and more.

Jenny   We are.

Richard   He says in some cases, we could compete with big glossy magazines, *Vanity Fair* and so forth.

Jenny   In some cases, yes. What's the problem?

Richard   The problem is, the big glossies are owned by very big corporations, and we're not.

Jenny   I know. We're owned by your savings.

Richard   Correction. We used to be owned by my savings. Now we're owned by my credit cards.

Jenny   God, already?

Richard   Already, God. So Michael wants to know how you can justify offering these people such exorbitant fees.

Jenny   Why would they write for us otherwise? We're nobodies.

Richard   I thought we were cutting-edge, day-after-tomorrow, new-paradigm nobodies.

Jenny   That's the plan.

Richard   So why don't we find some like-minded, talented cutting-edge nobodies we don't have to pay so much?

Jenny   Because we need some relatively established names so people will visit the site so advertisers will think it worthwhile to advertise so that some day one day we can make a profit. And for now, we have to pay over the odds to get people to write for us at all.

Richard (*to us*)   And how was that different from getting some Seamus Heaney in there?

Jenny   This is a new economy, Richard, with new ways of doing business, new paradigms. And you say you believe that, you sing it out loud, and then every time you come away from one of those sneering fucks, Michael and Gerry, you're full of doubt and despair and how will we make the few shillings out of this. I mean, when did either of those middle-aged schoolboys ever take a risk in his life?

Richard   You're right.

Jenny (*to us*)   Gerry is a solicitor who took over his father's practice when his father retired. Michael is an accountant who blah blah blah when *his* father died. They both have huge houses by the sea and holiday homes in the west and wives who gave up their careers to raise the kids.

Richard (*to us*)   Michael and Gerry did very well for themselves all right, fair play to them. (*To* **Jenny**.) We must have them over some time. And their wives.

Jenny   They don't really like you, Richard.

Richard   Who doesn't? Michael and Gerry's wives? I get along really well with Caroline and . . . and –

Jenny   Annabel. No. Michael and Gerry don't really like you.

Richard   I don't really like them either. But they're my oldest friends, so what can you do? We were at primary school together.

Jenny   They sneer at you.

Richard   I sneer at them.

Jenny   They think you're a loser.

Richard   They may be right. But if it doesn't work out: a) I can always go back to making the world safe for bloated white plutocrats, and b) there's money set aside in your account to pay the mortgage for months yet. So we won't be on the side of the road.

Jenny   We knew we were going to go into debt.

Richard   I just thought we had a little more leeway. My fault. I've a hit list of potential investors, I'll set up some meetings.

Jenny   Do you need me along?

Richard   I'll fly solo, no problem.

Jenny   'Cause it's kind of tight here, making sure we've enough content for the launch –

Richard   She needed to focus on her job and leave me to do mine. Which was trying to keep us afloat. Expenses had been mounting: domain registration, web hosting, pizza for Peter and Andy, the fucking telephone bill, and now the contributors' fees had sent us into the red. But we didn't lose our faith.

Jenny   We were building up a wealth of cutting-edge content: science and technology, money, celebrity, pornography, the forces that shape the way we live now, at the end of the American Century, we citizens of 51st State.

Richard The 51st State Brand is our Brand, it reflects us back to ourselves in all our interconnectedness, our newness, our nowness.

Jenny The truth lies in the near future. Body and soul braced for adventure, for revelation – isn't that the time you feel most alive? As opposed to the backward drift, the listless slide and wallow, Mammy and Daddy and that old shit.

Richard My mother is dying.

Jenny She's been dying for years.

Richard She's not got long now. I wish you'd go see her.

Jenny Stella doesn't want to see me, Richard. She never did.

Richard I don't think that's true. All right, she's not the easiest of women.

Jenny That's one way of putting it.

Richard But she has her reasons. Something happened.

Jenny Did it? What?

Richard I don't know. A long time ago. Something.

Pause.

Jenny Kevin got in the habit of dropping in.

Jenny *is drinking. So is* **Kevin**.

Richard Nearly every day, it seemed.

Jenny We'd talk for hours.

Kevin The problem is, economists and business-heads listen to working people arguing for higher wages and they go: there you are, everyone's out for what he can get, we're all the same, we'd all love to be millionaires. But that's bullshit: there's a minimum you need in the way of food and shelter and so on, then there's a little more you want so you're not exhausted and desperate trying to grind out the necessities, and then there's a basic level of security you should have so you can't be put out on the street on the whim of some board of directors who want higher profits that quarter for the shareholders and your family is going to have to suffer. Now if you want more, if you want to be a millionaire, good for you. But don't turn round and tell me that's what I want as well. I don't want to be a millionaire, I don't want to be a poet, I want to be a teacher. You're saying: well, you can be a teacher, but you can't afford to have a house, or raise a family, or any of the normal things in life. You can be a teacher, but you'll never own a villa in Antigua, or a Lexus, or a Rolex watch, that's fine. I don't want to be the people I read about in magazines. I just want to be able to afford the fucking magazine. And are you saying to me, the only way to have a reasonable expectation of raising a family and living a life with any degree of modest comfort and security is to be a millionaire? Because if you are, then we are all well and truly fucked.

Jenny You're absolutely right, it's totally gross how materialistic everyone's become. I really despise this whole greedhead culture.

Kevin It's more than a culture, it's like a religion, like we all agreed to worship the Market as the one true Church.

Jenny I know, 'cause we all talk money talk now, and our money talks right back to us.

Kevin Yeah, it says: Lower Taxes plus Flexible Workforce plus Deregulation –

Jenny Plus Privatisation plus Globalisation equals The New Economy –

Kevin Equals True Democracy equals The Way Things Are, Now And For Ever –

Jenny And the Economists are our Priests, and Money Talk is our Liturgy, and Investments are our Sacraments –

Kevin   And the Almighty Market is, was, and for ever shall be, world without end –

Jenny   Amen.

Pause.

Richard   Kevin was here *again*? What do you find to talk about?

Jenny   You, Richard, and where we'll run away to once we've murdered you and hidden your corpse in the cellar.

Richard   That's funny.

Jenny   So is you cross-examining me. What's next, accusing?

Richard   You can hardly blame me for –

Jenny   Blaming, that's what's next. We're not those people any more, Richard, remember? We believed we could change.

Richard   I'm sorry.

Jenny   I can't keep apologising for one mistake.

Richard   I know, I know. (*Pause.*) We were both at fault. We both needed to change.

Jenny   We were sick of ourselves. I said, let's try being somebody else. It wasn't the worst dream.

Richard (*to us*)   It's just, being somebody else is easier dreamt than done.

Kevin   The moon hangs high above the ruined church. Yew and cypress stand in clusters amid the gorse. The vaulted cliffs of the quarry glow, like the damp walls of an old cathedral. Hard to dream the future, in a place so ancient and grave.

Richard (*to himself*)   History's finished. The future is now.

Jenny   Not that I wasn't tempted. He had a certain *allure*.
But I wanted Kevin to write for 51st State. I needed the new
material.

Kevin   It's not a poem, it's a story. A fable. About a gold
rush.

Jenny   That happened here?

Kevin   In the hills around the quarry. It climaxed with an
apparition, witnessed by hundreds: right above the ruined
church, the treasure seekers saw a blazing cross of fire.

Marion   I was just relieved that he was doing something
at last. And getting paid for it too.

Kevin   A crucifix of flame across the sky!

Jenny   Try not to make it too religious.

Marion   By the time I noticed there was something
wrong, he was completely obsessed by it all.

Jenny *and* **Richard**.

Richard   We were pushing ahead with the site – get it up
and running, and people would see what we meant. We
needed to advertise, and pay more contributors, we were
flat out –

Jenny   Up until four, and then up again at eight, seven
days a week; Peter the Programmer did his stuff, and Andy
put together an amazing-looking interface, kind of
medieval-oriental meets the future, but very millennial, very
now. You know what I mean?

Richard   The problem was, none of the suits I was trying
to extract investment from knew what Jenny meant. I wasn't
even sure I did.

Jenny   So what about J.J.?

Richard   I don't want to ask J.J.

Jenny   J.J. MacTaggert was a client of Richard's in
Atlanta. Georgia real-estate tycoon. Absolutely loaded.

Richard   Sure, investing a million dollars would make
about as big a dent in J.J.'s budget as buying a six-pack of
beer would make in mine, but that doesn't mean J.J.'s
happy to piss a million away.

Jenny   And then, Richard had a breakthrough.

Richard   The New Media UK Association were running
an Angel Investment Programme, and they had a round of
interviews in Dublin. The deal was, you auditioned before
three members of the association who had approved your
business plan. If you got past them –

Jenny   And he did –

Richard   You had to pitch your idea to a panel of eight
angel investors in London. And if you made the cut again –

Jenny   And he did –

Richard   Then you had a real shot, pitching to between
twenty and fifty actual investors – all totally excited by the
dot.com revolution, all genuinely eager to part with their
money, all warmed up and on your side.

Jenny   So at that stage, Richard said:

Richard   I can't do this without you. If anyone knows
what we're doing – knows *why* we're doing what we're doing
– it's you.

Enter **Kevin**.

Kevin   The vaulted cliffs of the granite quarry, like three
walls of a great cathedral. Our house where the fourth wall
should be. And the ruined church above us all.

*The sound of a phone line dialling and connecting to the Internet. A
laptop computer glows.*

Richard   51st State went online at midnight last night.
We had a party with Peter and Andy and Gerry and
Michael and all the gang; tonight it's Kevin and Marion.

Jenny *has been drinking. She pours fizz for* **Kevin** *and* **Richard**
and refills her ice-filled glass with liquor from a green bottle.

Jenny   Three thousand, seven hundred and forty-six hits
in eighteen hours!

She looks through some mail, picks one letter out, checks that
Richard *isn't looking, hides the letter underneath the laptop.*

Kevin *plugs the baby monitor in; gives* **Richard** *two bottles of
wine, looks at the laptop screen.*

Kevin   That's fantastic! Is it?

Richard   It's not bad. Where's Marion?

Kevin   Caught in traffic, I guess. That's where she usually
is.

Richard   God, west Dublin's a nightmare.

Jenny   That half a million people are trying to awake
from.

Richard   She's OK, is she? She's on a mobile?

Kevin   The battery must be dead. It's all right, folks, she's
two months to go yet.

Marion   My first contraction hit ten minutes after leaving
work. I thought, this can't be right, I've two months to go
yet.

Kevin   It *looks* amazing. (*Reads.*) '51st State: Neither here
nor there, but that space between.' Very good.

Jenny   He's mocking us.

Richard   He's praising you.

Jenny   That's *how* he mocks us, Richard. With faintly
insincere praise.

Richard   Why should he mock us? He's doing a piece for us, isn't he?

Kevin   I am indeed, Richard.

Richard   Why wasn't it ready for the launch issue?

Jenny   Not your department, Richard!

Kevin   I still have a lot of research to do.

Marion   I thought, another contraction and I'll just drive straight to the maternity ward. But I was two miles past the hospital when the second crashed in.

Kevin   '51st Thought: The New Medievalism: in a Corporate World, we are all Serfs now.' I do like the sound of that, actually.

Richard   I hate that piece.

Jenny   You haven't even read it, Richard.

Richard   I don't need to read it. I don't want to read it.

Kevin   Why not, Richard?

Richard   Because it's anti-business.

Jenny   'Anti-business'? Jesus.

Kevin   '51st Tech: Companies the New Government, Internet the New Democracy.' I'm guessing that would be pro-business?

Richard   Just common sense, Kevin.

Jenny   You're turning into a bloated white plutocrat, Richard.

Richard   Here's hoping!

Kevin   '51st Sex: "A Bloody Tale" – Confessions of a Sexual Vampire'; '51st Crime: Women kill 'cause they're Bad, not Mad'; '51st Biotech: Design your children, reconfigure yourself – the ultimate pill.'

Marion   Two more contractions, ten minutes between now. Wasn't really in shape for thinking. Seemed easier to drive straight home.

Jenny   You don't like it, Kevin.

Kevin   It's very impressive. It's kind of scary though, isn't it? Who's La Sanguinara?

Richard   She's a vampire.

Jenny   She's an eminent member of the intravenous community.

Richard   Would you hang around, check out the articles?

Kevin   I suppose I would. If I was online.

Jenny   Luddite stopout that you are.

Kevin   How did it go in London then? Did you get the investment you needed?

Richard   Fine.

Jenny   No.

Richard   It went OK.

Jenny   It didn't go OK. We didn't get the investment we needed.

Richard   It'll be OK. We'll get there, Kevin, now the old site's up and running.

Kevin   No doubt about that –

Jenny   We had a row.

Richard   Jenny.

Jenny   OK, married couple has a row not front-page news agree with you. We had, however, prior to our private row, a public disagreement when we were pitching. To the investors, the panel of angel investors, Kevin.

Richard   Slight difference of emphasis.

Jenny   Fundamental, Richard, fundamental.

Richard   Teething trouble. Never know how you're going to respond until people show an interest, Kevin.

Jenny   But we rehearsed the pitch together, Richard. The only reason I was there to express the meaning of 51st State. What it means. Richard.

Kevin   If you guys'd prefer not to talk about this –

Jenny   No, no. Au contraire.

Richard   I'd prefer not to talk about it.

Jenny   No one's asking you to, Richard. The hotel. Holiday Inn off a motorway. Conference room. Bowls of fruit, bottles of water. Fifty investors waiting for us.

Richard   Forty-six.

Jenny   They have their little packs, you got one, Kevin, with the business plan and the costings and the graphics and the logo and a T-shirt and everything.

Richard   They loved the packs. They commented on the packs.

Jenny   So. Richard says Internet dot.com e-commerce blah blah blah content still king first-class writers blah, and I say new reality Irish rate of change fastest in world traditions vanishing the future to be decided everything up for grabs 51st State to define cultural agenda for a new millennium. Questions.
And some little troll stands up and says, what about Seamus Heaney?

Richard   He didn't say that.

Jenny   He as good as.

Richard   He said, there's a huge ex-pat Irish community scattered across the globe: why not appeal specifically to them? And a lot of people nodded at this. And Jenny said the whole Irish thing was over, really, that people would soon cease to define themselves in narrow nationalistic terms, that 51st State was based in Ireland, but was a thoroughly global phenomenon.

Jenny That's right. And it *is* right.

Richard Yeah, but heads started shaking. Brows furrowed. No one really knew what you were talking about. So then this guy who'd asked the original question said if we managed to get some original work from the really famous Irish writers –

Jenny Of course, and the troll who said we should have some Seamus Heaney was *Richard*!

Richard I said we had access to some of his new, unpublished work –

Jenny A complete fantasy.

Richard But one they all – well, the few who'd heard of him – got excited by. Until, well –

Jenny Until I said 51st State was not about Celtic this or Irish that, and it had no intention of having anything to do with Seamus Heaney.

Richard And that was that, really; we ended up looking like a pair of fucking fools who didn't know what they were doing.

Jenny Whereas the reality *is* . . . (*Pause.*) Kevin.

Kevin Jenny.

Jenny You're a poet. Do you like Seamus Heaney, Kevin?

Kevin I do indeed, yes.

Jenny Do you really?

Kevin I think he's brilliant. I think he's a genius, actually.

Jenny I don't.

Richard   He won the Nobel Prize, Jenny.

Kevin   Heaney has this beautiful poem about the death of his mother. It's a memory of the two of them peeling potatoes together –

Jenny   Well, you see, that's what we've had enough of, Kevin, dead mammies and peeling potatoes and farms and bogs and fucking . . . all that old tweedy fucking . . .

Kevin   It's a very moving poem, actually.

Jenny   It's a tweedy little poem. Seamus Heaney is made of tweed.

Richard   Jenny.

Jenny   Tweedy little man with his tweedy little poems, and his spuds are all made of tweed tweed tweed –

Richard   Jenny, what are you drinking?

Jenny   Absinthe.

Richard   *Absinthe?* Jesus Christ. Where did you get absinthe?

Jenny   One of the techy boys gave it me last night.

Richard   Fuck sake, absinthe!

Kevin   It's sixty per cent proof, isn't it?

Jenny   Seventy.

Richard   Are you out of your mind?

Jenny   I am *now*.

Enter **Marion**.

Marion   Hi, guys. Sorry I'm so late. Kevin . . .

Kevin   Marion, what's the matter?

Marion   I've been having contractions all the way home. They're coming at five-minute intervals now. It's probably a false alarm, but . . . Richard, are you all right to drive? Or I can get a cab.

Richard   I'm good to go. Now?

Marion   Now'd be good. Kevin, my bag is packed, under –

Kevin   The bed in our room. See you at the car.

Marion   What about Baby Thomas?

Jenny (*stands up*)   Don't worry 'bout a thing. I can babysit. Safe in the hands of Auntie Jenny.

Jenny *falls over.*

Kevin   I'll get Mrs Patterson. She's offered loads of times.

Kevin *grabs the baby monitor and exits.*

Marion   Well done on 51st State, you two, it's absolutely excellent.

Richard   Thanks very much. Hear that, Jenny?

Jenny (*still on the floor*)   Yes. Thank you.

Marion   Everyone at work was talking about it. You should be really proud of yourselves.

Jenny   Oh, we are. Aren't we, Richard?

Richard   If we're not now, we never will be. All right, better go.

Jenny   Good luck, Marion! A little girl this time? Or another boy?

Marion   You decide.

Jenny   Girl please!

Exit **Richard** *and* **Marion**. **Jenny** *hauls herself upright and follows them out.*

The sound, off, of car doors slamming and a car revving and driving away at speed.

*Enter **Jenny**. She sits at the laptop computer and retrieves the letter she hid beneath it.*

Jenny   'Dear Ms Ryan, RE: Standing Order blah blah blah, we wish to bring to your attention . . .' (*Pause.*) Oh fuck *off*!

She tosses the letter in the bin.

The light in the room has dimmed now as night has fallen.

*The computer screen lights **Jenny**'s face.*

If we're not now, we never will be.

She hits the off switch, and the stage goes black.

Act Two

Richard *and* **Marion**.

Richard   At Christmas, everyone was expected to sing, but the real party began when my mother was called upon for a second time. I'd creep down and watch from the stairs as she'd run through what she called her late-night repertoire: 'Blues in the Night', 'I'll Remember April', 'All The Things You Are', and her favourite, 'Alone Together', and my aunts and uncles would applaud fiercely, and my father would nearly always cry, and my mother would catch him in the act of wiping a furtive tear away and instantly she would launch into 'The Gentleman is a Dope', and he'd stand and take a bow, and then they'd duet on 'The Folks Who Live on the Hill', and all my aunts would cry, and one of my uncles would spy me and I'd be hauled into the living room, and asked to lead the company in a carol, and I'd always choose 'Have Yourself a Merry Little Christmas', and we'd all sing the first chorus and leave my mother to sing the rest, and of course when she'd reach the part about how someday soon we all would be together, if the fates allow, *everyone* would cry, because Grandad was not long dead, and my mother would hug me tight, and I knew that nothing was ever going to go wrong. And then . . . something happened.

Marion   What happened? You should ask her, Richard.

Richard   Once they were happy, suddenly she never would be again, The End. That's what Jenny said.

Marion   Except it wasn't the end.

Richard   No, it wasn't. I was about ten or so when everything changed. My mother never sang again, and eventually, I stopped trying to persuade her. She would sit in a darkened room – from then on, it seemed as if the curtains were always drawn – and smoke, and play patience, and listen to her Jo Stafford records. She still dressed as she always had, as if expecting guests: full make-up, painted finger and toenails, needle-creased trouser suits and twinsets, strappy sling-back high heels – but no guests ever called. My father would come home from work, then pad about in a cardigan and slippers doing the housework. There were days when she'd just stay in bed. An omelette would be ferried up on a tray. If not, then the darkened room, the pack of cards, the Jo Stafford. Sometimes we'd all play: gin rummy, or whist. Mostly, she'd play alone. My father would sit alone in the kitchen, reading westerns and drinking bottles of ale. And I would be alone in my bedroom, waiting.

Marion *and* **Kevin**.

Kevin   As soon as Marion sat in Richard's car, the contractions stopped. By the time we hit Monkstown, we knew it was a false alarm.

Marion   It had been another bad day at work. Three months earlier, NPK had decided to shed twenty per cent of staff worldwide. That meant firing people I'd been working with for years. And one of the benefits of owning stock was, I got to fire most of them myself. 'NPK's profits are your profits': that was the deal. The logic seemed impeccable: efficiency, rationalisation, a newer, leaner company. Only problem was, we simply couldn't cope. We had too much work, and we couldn't finish it on time. We started to lose contracts we'd always had first refusal on. We'd let the company know of our concerns, and that morning, we got NPK's response: fire another ten per cent.

Kevin   I'll phone the school.

Marion   Don't. Not this year, anyway. It's good for Thomas to be with his dad every day.

Kevin   But if NPK go under –

Marion   Kevin, NPK are a massive global concern, they're not just going to 'go under'.

Kevin   I guess not.

Marion   The next two months at work were pretty rough. But I kept thinking, whatever happens, don't let it affect the baby.

Kevin   In the end, the birth was two weeks late.

Marion   A little girl: Angelica.

Kevin   Marion was exhausted at first, but she soon recovered: the baby slept six hours through the night from the second week. And Thomas was excited that his mummy was around all the time.

Marion *hushes* **Kevin**, *switches on monitor.*

Marion   That's her down now.

Kevin   I'll read Thomas a story.

Marion   Too late.

Kevin   He's asleep already? But it's only seven, he never goes to bed before half.

Marion   He was shattered.

Kevin   Well, if he's up at the crack of dawn –

Marion   Then he can keep me and Angelica company. What's wrong?

Kevin   I would have done bath time.

Marion   You're angry 'cause I'm giving you some time off.

Kevin   You won't let me help at all.

Marion   There are men who dream of wives like me.

Kevin   I'm not joking.

Marion   But I am, so you'll understand how silly you're being. Leave the house unaccompanied. It's fun when you remember how.

Kevin   But I want to help –

Marion   Well, you could learn to drive. Then you could go to the supermarket on your own. Or you could take charge of the washing. We're on two loads a day now, and it's hard keeping up with it all. There's two ways you could help.

Pause.

Kevin   When are you going back to work?

Marion   What?

Kevin   It's just a question.

Marion   I went back three weeks after Thomas was born –

Kevin   You couldn't get out of here quick enough then –

Marion   Well, this time it's different. I'm really enjoying being round the house, spending time with the baby and with Thomas. If that's a problem for you, Kevin –

Kevin   It's not a problem –

Marion   Good. How's your gold-rush story coming? I can't wait to see it, it sounds –

Kevin   Why is it so important to you that I write this story?

Marion   I don't know. It sounds really interesting.

Kevin   You didn't think that when Aimee turned it down.

Marion   Well, I didn't know enough about it then. I do now. I'm interested in your work.

Kevin   Are you? You never used to be. When my work was teaching, you weren't interested at all.

Marion   That's because the only times you'd ever mention it were to moan about teaching the same topics year after year, or whinge about how boring all the other teachers were, or whine about how badly paid you were –

Kevin   Moan, whinge, whine, how attractive I must have been –

Marion   On top of which, the last year at the school you were pissed all the time, so yes, I might have rolled my eyes occasionally, 'cause it was pretty clear you weren't happy.

Kevin   The way I remember it, you were riddled with guilt about selling out and joining the corporate greedheads, so you decided I should keep the flag of integrity flying for both of us, I should give up teaching and become a writer on the basis of one poem –

Marion   It's not just one poem, you used to write book reviews and articles for those magazines –

Kevin   Those little magazines with a circulation limited to however many friends and relations the contributors had, that's like amateur acting, Marion, it's a leisure activity, not a profession; the point is, you want me to compensate for you, because deep down you despise what you do –

Marion   No, deep down, I despise – I don't like – what you've been doing. Despite your insistence that you've been this blissful stay-at-home dad since Thomas was born, you still pass out drunk on the sofa five nights out of seven, you're grumpy and sullen and sour about everyone who actually has a go and does something, you're never done sneering at Richard and shouting at the television, and maybe I'm wrong, maybe you don't want to write, but anything is better than sitting around getting drunk and feeling sorry for yourself –

Kevin   I've been looking after Thomas –

Marion   I know you have, and you do it really brilliantly, and it's beautiful to see the two of you together. But it's not enough for you, and no amount of insisting it is will make it so.

Pause.

Kevin   We've really got to think about baptism, Marion.

Marion   What?

Kevin   About getting the children baptised.

Marion   Do we? And what religion do we think they might be baptised into? Shall we just pick one at random?

Kevin   Well, I'm a Catholic.

Marion   I'm not. You're lapsed –

Kevin   I'm not lapsed.

Marion   You haven't been in a church since we were married.

Kevin   I'm not lapsed, I'm just . . . out of practice.

Marion   Your favourite prayer was: 'Jesus, I know God doesn't exist, but could you put in a word for me anyway?'

Kevin (*short pause*)   I think that shows a certain quality of faith.

Marion (*short pause*)   Maybe once they're old enough, if we wanted to send them to a Catholic school –

Kevin   They need something more, don't you understand? Something more than just us. Than just this.

Marion   No, you need something more than just this, Kevin, and I wish you'd bloody find it, and stop tormenting yourself and everyone else.

Jenny *and* **Richard**.

Jenny   51st State was nominated as best newcomer at the European Web Awards in Leipzig. But at Dublin airport, all of Richard's credit cards failed. We had to come home on the bus.

Richard   Even with the site up, and rave reviews all over, we still couldn't get anyone to invest. We'd get advertisers for a month or so, then they'd slope off, and we'd spend all our time chasing them for payment. And we needed staff, and offices, and –

Jenny   Salaries. The supermarket was looking increasingly implausible. Not to mention the phone bill. So I decided there was only one thing for it: J.J.

Richard   I don't think we should.

Jenny   Why? Because if 51st State fails, you could always go back and work for him? Then go back now, Richard, 'cause we're broke.

Richard   We haven't failed.

Jenny   No we haven't. We've created a beautiful thing. We just need time to let it grow. And time means money. Anyway, he'll probably say no. Everyone else has.

Richard   OK, let's do it. 51st State!

Jenny   I sent J.J. MacTaggert all our investor bumf, with a personal letter from Richard, and a few days later I called him, at his offices on the eighty-seventh floor of the MacTaggert Building in Atlanta, Georgia. And got patched straight through to the great man.

Richard   And?

Jenny   J.J. said he didn't know what any of this dot.com business was except that it was a business, and if Richard managed it like he managed J.J.'s tax affairs, well, he wasn't gonna say it was a sure thing 'cause the one sure thing in this life is, ain't no such thing as a sure thing, but it's as close as it comes, and only a fool doesn't learn that close as it comes is as good as you get.

Richard   And?

Jenny   He said he'd put up the money.

Richard   51st State! (*Short pause.*) How much money?

Jenny   Five hundred.

Richard   You're kidding me.

Jenny   Yes I am. No I'm not. He said he'd put up five hundred and then look at things after a year.

Richard   Six months.

Jenny   No, he said a year.

Richard   But we're going to need more investment after six months, at the latest, there's no way we'll be turning a profit by then. Did you not say that?

Jenny   No I didn't; I said, J.J., you the man: will I put some Seamus Heaney in?

Richard   Did you?

Jenny   Richard, I doubt J.J. knows who Seamus Heaney is.

Richard   A year is too long.

Jenny   Six months is half a year more than we had this morning.

Richard   I'll have to talk to him.

Jenny   He's expecting you to call. But I don't think he'll change his mind. You know J.J.

Richard   What do you mean, 'You know J.J.'?

Jenny   What?

Richard   What do you mean: 'You know J.J.'?

Jenny   Whatever, I don't know. You know J.J., what he's like.

Richard   I know I do. I've known him for five years. The point is, that's the first time you ever spoke to him.

Jenny   So?

Richard   So *you* don't . . . oh, nothing.

Jenny   No, say it: I don't *what*?

Richard   Nothing. It doesn't matter.

Jenny   Nothing.

Richard   Nothing.

Pause.

Jenny   Just phone him, OK.

Exit **Jenny**.

Richard   So is it the getting of wisdom or the death of desire? Because five years ago, we'd've been into it hammer and tongs, screaming and yelling, tears and slammed doors and the whole bloody libretto, and then making up hours later with some frenzied, tear-stained fuck on the floor. But now, we bite our lips and hold our tongues. 'Don't go there.' That's what we say. We used to go there all the time, crawl into each other's heads and spin them till they jangled, nerves frayed and senses shaken, marriage like a roiling fever. We don't go there any more. Which is change. Which is good, of course, change is good. We've grown up a little, we trust each other more. Although sometimes it feels like, having stopped going there, we've lost something. Sometimes, now, it feels like we never go anywhere.

Marion *and* **Kevin**.

Marion   I'd talk once a week with Dave Johnson at Ferguson Gough, as NPK still let us call it, although it was a completely different company now. Dave said things were hell, but things were fine, they had stabilised, no need to worry. And that was just as well, 'cause I wasn't in the least worried. I was living in milky baby heaven, nappies and teddies, cuddles and squalls, everything I'd somehow failed to connect with first time round.

Kevin   I miss my little boy.

Marion   You take him on walks every morning, you do bedtime most nights, when he wakes up he calls for you first.

Jesus, it isn't as if I've kidnapped him. I'm just trying to make up for lost time.

Kevin   When we're out he keeps asking for you.

Marion   And is that bad? This should be such a happy time, Kevin, for us all, for the family, but you're ruining it with your constant whining.

Kevin   I'm not whining, I'm just . . . trying to adjust.

Marion   Well, could you manage it without being such an epic pain in the hole? When I was working long hours you never let up on how Thomas missed me and needed to see me, now I'm here every day, you're jealous of the time I spend with him. Well, I am not going to apologise for being in my own house and looking after my own children. Except I thought I only had two of them to deal with, not three.

Kevin (*to us*)   She was right, of course. My world had shrunk. Now Marion had taken charge, I felt I had been cut loose. And all that was left was the quarry, the yew trees and the cypress, the wind blowing down the hill from the ruined church.

Richard *and* **Jenny**.

Richard   We paid back debts, we rented office space, we hired staff.

Jenny   We were nominated for three more awards, and won one: *NetSurf* magazine – Best New Site.

Richard   We seemed to do a lot of entertaining – at least, Jenny did –

Jenny   All part of the job: new projects to be commissioned, fresh contacts to be made.

Richard   And flights, and hotels –

Jenny   It wasn't like they were jaunts, it was business every time, Richard.

Richard   No, that's right. Only – well, Michael said what I'd been thinking myself: don't confuse investment with profit. We were basically pouring J.J.'s money down the toilet.

Jenny   No, we were proceeding like a normal business –

Richard   Michael said, of course, the problem is, Richard, dot.coms aren't normal businesses. If they were, no one would've invested in any of them at all, 'cause the prospect of profit is dim. And there may soon come a day of reckoning.

Jenny   The fuck does he know? Baldy old tweedboy. Look at the Nasdaq, Richard, it's untouchable. Everything's changed. The new paradigm. Remember? Don't bail out now we finally have some money. We're winning prizes, Richard, glittering prizes.

Richard   I thought: don't confuse investment with profit. I said: you're absolutely right.

Jenny   What we dreamed of, we're doing. This is us, doing it. We'll get more investment. We'll get advertising. Hell, we'll even make a –

Richard   Don't say it.

Jenny   I will say it. PROFIT!

Richard   And for a few weeks . . . shit, everyone loved us, we were the hottest thing, why shouldn't it've worked? It *was* working. And it was all down to Jenny. It was her dream.

Jenny   It was the adventure of our lives.

Richard   And all the while, my mother was dying.

Marion *gives* **Richard** *a wrapped gift.*

Marion   Cologne for your mum.

Richard   Thank you. She'll like that. (*Short pause.*) God, Marion, she's just slipping away. Slipping out of reach.

Marion   Richard, try your best to find out . . . just what it was that happened to her.

Richard   After my father died, my mother began to apply herself to her drinking: vodka, a bottle a day. The doctor says there's no cancer, no heart disease, no pulmonary disorders, but that her body can only take so much abuse. But Jenny was right. My mother's been dying for years. And only she knows why.

Jenny   Richard's house was like something from *Sunset Boulevard*: the curtains always drawn, the fruity smell of booze, the framed photographs of Stella singing with some big band in Torquay, the Jo Stafford records on twenty-four-hour rotation. The first thing she ever said to me was, would you like a cocktail? Then she asked me if I knew Jo Stafford was a Catholic convert. Then when we were leaving, she told Richard I was obviously an alcoholic.

Richard   What must we do for the dying? Leave them be. That's what my mother said she wanted. 'Away and leave me be.' But she had patience to play, and smoking and drinking to get through, and Jo Stafford records to listen to. And then she couldn't do the patience, the records, the drinking and the smoking. She wasn't up to them any more. What could we do for her then? She'd say: 'Leave me alone.' There's a big difference between 'Leave me be' and 'Leave me alone.' Leave me be, I've still got some living to do. Leave me alone, I'm better off dead. So that's what we must do for the dying. Sooner or later, we must leave them alone.

Jenny   I was sad for Richard. But Stella made it clear from the off that she despised me. Frankly, we couldn't leave her alone soon enough.

Kevin *and* **Marion**.

Marion   And then Dave Johnson rang and said things were hell and they were not fine really and did I think there was any way I could make it back into the office. I had only taken four weeks leave at this stage. But as a stockholder, the company's profits were my lookout.

(Part of the problem with employees becoming stockholders is, all you think about is maximising the company's share value, 'cause that increases your salary. So you never have an excuse to knock off work. You become the boss who enforces inhuman hours upon yourself, at the expense of family life, social life, life. You become your own jailer.)

So I went back to what was left of Ferguson Gough. A whole raft of staff had had enough, and just walked. Of seven senior designers, only Dave and I remained. It didn't make any sense, we barely had enough people left to run an office, let alone tender for and execute design contracts. We weren't even being asked to pitch for the work any more. The word was out: they're not up to it. But we were getting the same old mantra from NPK: efficiency, rationalisation, a newer, leaner company. Just, there's a limit to how lean you can get, before you're pared right down to the bone.

Jenny *at her laptop. Enter* **Richard**.

Jenny   How is she?

Richard   She's only a few days left. I wish you'd go see her.

Jenny   She wouldn't want to see me.

Richard   That isn't what I said.

Jenny   Michael called.

Richard   Yes, he called me too. To say you had fired him.

Jenny   That wasn't quite how I put it –

Richard   That's how he took it. And that, despite my best efforts at dissuasion and blandishment, is how it is.

Jenny   He's just a fucking accountant, Richard. We can always get another one.

Richard   Where are we going to find one who doesn't charge us for a year's work? Who tries to help us to stay afloat by finding opportunities for us, only to be thanked by my wife telling him to fuck off.

Jenny   I didn't say fuck off. Well, I did, but I didn't mean . . . I meant more: Fuck away off out of that, than Fuck off.

Richard   He didn't get the distinction.

Jenny   He doesn't get anything. Don't come snivelling in here about poor Michael, the guy has nothing but derision, contempt, actually, for me, for 51st State, for everything we're trying to do here.

Richard   He knows the hole we're in. He's trying to help us dig our way out of it.

Jenny   By finding you private accountancy clients? Didn't think I knew about that, did you?

Richard   We need some cash flow that isn't investment. We're nearly through J.J.'s stake, with no more on the horizon, no advertising worth talking about . . . I mean, why can't you acknowledge the state we're in?

Jenny   I know it's bad.

Richard   You rang the accountancy clients Michael secured for me, clients of his own that he was generous enough to offer to stop us from going under, you rang them and told them it was all a mistake.

Jenny   Yes.

Richard   Don't you understand a thing? Everything is falling apart. We don't have any money.

Jenny   And if you jump ship to become an accountant again –

Richard   It wouldn't be jumping ship –

Jenny   Of course it would. You'd just drop me in it, say, well, too bad, nice while it lasted but it was only a dream.

Richard   Isn't that what we're going to have to say?

Jenny   Richard, this is the adventure of our lives. Are you going to bail out before you can honestly say you gave it your best shot?

Richard   No. But –

Jenny   Things are turning, I can feel it. Two pieces got reprinted by American dailies last week, we get a fee for that, I know, a pittance, but that's credibility, Richard, that's a status you can't just ignore.

Richard   This is the adventure of our lives?

Jenny   Well, it is. Don't you want to stay on board?

Richard   Until we hit the rocks?

Jenny   Until we leverage 51st State into success. One last push: the market survey confirmed 51st State has an audience profile almost exclusively composed of high-value users, didn't it? That's got to up the attraction where advertisers are concerned.

Richard   I've no budget left. When I said I had no money, I wasn't talking like an accountant, who thinks he has no money when he's only ten grand left in the bank. I mean I don't have the money to pay anyone this month. Including ourselves.

Jenny   I have some cash flow left from the contributors' fund.

Richard   Will that cover staff salaries too?

Jenny   Just about. One last push? And I'll call Michael and apologise and grovel.

Richard   This is the adventure of our lives.

Jenny   I'm so proud of you.

Richard (*to us*)   I was such a fucking fool. How could she have had that much money in a contributors' fund? I should have called the bank there and then and found out where the money was coming from. I should have bloody *known*. But I was in too deep. I was co-dependent. And what with visiting my mother every day, and sitting with her, and being able to do nothing . . . *nothing* . . . I needed to trust Jenny. To let her take some of the strain.

Jenny   We had to push to the end. I know I shouldn't have . . . but so many dot.coms were starting to turn around when their owners lost their nerve and pulled the plug. I didn't want us sitting around saying, 'We nearly made it. We might've been.' Even if it meant losing everything.

Richard   And there was something in her eyes that had always made me feel we were jumping off a cliff together . . . and that she had a way of landing safely.

Exit **Richard** *and* **Jenny**.

Marion *and* **Kevin**.

Marion   I arrived at the business park one morning to find NPK's doors locked. Dave Johnson and I huddled in a canteen and watched our fate unfold on CNN. The *Washington Post* had reported that NPK International had raided their employees' pension funds to divert moneys into failing wings of the NPK conglomerate and to invest in assorted dot.com enterprises, all of them ill-fated. The company had lost billions in the process. NPK stock was going to be delisted from the Dow. Employee pensions were completely worthless. Dave started to cry. I cried with him, gave him a hug and drove home.

Kevin   The bank called before Marion made it through the door. Her last two months' salary hadn't gone through. Yesterday's mortgage payment meant we were majorly overdrawn.

Marion   Where's Thomas? And Angelica?

Kevin   They're with Mrs Patterson. Thomas is helping her bake a chocolate cake.

Marion   You'd better call the school.

Kevin   I have. They've appointed someone; I'll have to wait until September next year.

Marion   I don't believe this. What are we going to do? Oh Kevin, hold me.

Kevin *and* **Marion** *embrace.*

Kevin   It's the will of God.

Marion   What's that?

Kevin   The will of God. Indifferent, relentless, like the wind. No sense in trying to resist it. Just got to let it . . . blow through our coats.

Marion *(to us)*   'The will of God'? I nodded, and hugged him, and cried, and then we went and got the kids and played with them, and tried not to think about any of it. But . . . 'the will of God'. That was the first sign for me. Though when I finally saw the gold-rush story, I understood it had been brewing for a while.

Richard.

Richard   On the last day she could speak, my mother said: 'Jenny's wrong. I don't think she's not good enough for you. I see she thinks you're not good enough for her. And that's no recipe for happiness.' And she said: 'You know she's an alcoholic, don't you?' And I said: 'Yes, Mammy, I know.' And I said: 'What happened, Mammy? Why did you stop singing?' And of course, what happened was, nothing – slow and relentless, the pale, day-to-day nothing of a frustrated, vain, bored suburban housewife, fitfully scorched by the occasional, sputtering flash of what might have been – hearing a song she used to sing on the radio, or seeing a poster for her old band on tour with a new featured female singer, or the mere mention of the word 'Torquay', where she had played three summer seasons – phantoms of a shadow life, the life she could never lead, the life that would haunt her all her days. And so, gradually, and then suddenly, nothing. And so it soon became easier to drink than not, to remain silent than sing, to turn away than reach out.

That was what happened. Once they were happy, suddenly they never would be again, The End.

And my mother said: 'Sing "Alone Together".' So I did.

He sings the first verse (he can hold a tune).

And she said: 'I don't know where it went, your father could hold a tune too, but you, son. You haven't a note, God love you.' And she nodded off. As I was leaving, she awoke, and said: 'You're making out all right, aren't you, son?' I said: 'No need to worry about me, Mammy.' And she smiled. The next morning, they gave her morphine. Her jaw fell slack as she slept, and her upper false teeth kept slipping, so I would replace them. She had more morphine later on. I spent most of the day adjusting her teeth, and wiping her brow, and freshening her make-up. I know she would have wanted to look her best. And then gradually, the gap between her breathing in and breathing out got longer and longer. Until the artery in her neck stopped moving. That meant she was dead. (*Pause.*) No need to worry about me, Mammy.

Exit **Richard**.

Enter **Jenny** *and* **Kevin**. **Jenny** *is drunk.* **Kevin** *plugs the monitor in.* **Jenny** *flicks quickly through some mail, whips one letter out and stows it away, as before, under the laptop.*

Jenny   Could Mrs Patterson not've taken the kids?

Kevin   She wanted to go to the funeral. It's all right, it's just Angelica, Marion's taken Thomas to the park.

Jenny   Have a drink?

Kevin   It's not absinthe, is it?

Jenny   Oh God, never again. It's gin. I wasn't so drunk that night, was I? The absinthe night?

Kevin   You were, actually.

Jenny   Was I? I thought I got away with it.

Kevin   Well. You didn't die. Sorry.

Jenny   Sorry, why? Oh, bad taste day that's the type of thing. Yeah, well, we never got along. She was a total bitch to me, in fact. Richard said something had happened to make her like that. He didn't know what, though. And frankly, I don't care. There's simply no excuse for bad manners.

Pause.

Kevin   Richard took it pretty hard.

Jenny   Of course. Poor Richard. Still. Had to get out of that bloody hotel. Now.

Kevin   Thanks.

Jenny   Cheers! That's better.

Kevin   Christ, that's strong.

Jenny   Gin, with a little gin in it. God, that awful bloody priest.

Kevin   He was all right.

Jenny   He sang 'All The Things You Are'.

Kevin   He lilted a few lines.

Jenny   He sang a verse and chorus.

Kevin   In tribute, like. To her love of Jo Stafford.

Jenny   I know why he did it. I just don't know what gave him the nerve.

Kevin   Ah well. God rest her anyhow. And all the dead. (*Pause.*) Time for Angelica's feed, I'd better get back.

Jenny   No, no, stay. She's fine, sure, she's still asleep. Have another drink.

Kevin   I still have this one, thanks.

Jenny   Well, I'm having another. And what about some music? Swear there'd be a funeral or something.

Kevin   Were all the people from the website there?

Jenny   Oh yes. And Gerry and Michael, and their awful bloody wives. 'Oh, Jenny, your website, you're so *brave*.' They kept calling it 51st *Stage*. As if it was a fucking bus stop. Stuck-up cunts. Ah, the very thing. This was our theme song at college.

Kevin   You and Richard?

Jenny   God, *no*. Me and my *friends*. It's called 'Getting Away With It'.

She plays the record – 'Getting Away With It' by Electronic. She kicks off her shoes and dances about. She shouts over the music.

It's very eighties, I'm afraid. But you are what you are, isn't that right, Kevin?

Kevin   I suppose so.

Jenny *sings along to the chorus.*

Jenny   'I've been getting away with it all my life.' Come on, dance!

She turns the music up.

Kevin   I'm not really much of a dancer.

Jenny   Oh, I bet you are.

Kevin   Honestly, I'm not.

Jenny   Well. You don't have to be. It's eighties dancing. You just jump about and wave your arms like a fool.

Kevin   I'd really rather not.

Jenny   Oh Jesus, Kevin, don't be so fucking pompous.

Jenny *takes* **Kevin***'s hands, pulls him to her. They dance awkwardly for a while, then* **Jenny** *stumbles, knocking* **Kevin** *over and falling on top of him. Gin goes everywhere.*

Enter **Richard**. *He stares at* **Jenny** *and* **Kevin** *on the floor, picks up the remote control and stops the music. Over the monitor, the sound of the baby crying.*

Kevin *has leapt to his feet.*

Kevin   Richard –

Richard   It's all right, Kevin.

Pause.

Kevin   The baby. I'd better go.

Exit **Kevin**.

Richard *gets a cloth and begins to wipe up the spilt gin.* **Jenny** *is suddenly very drunk.*

Jenny   Richard.

Richard   What?

Jenny   I am *so* sorry.

Richard   Are you? What for?

Jenny   I just wanted to play a record. (*Immediately on the defensive again.*) Why, what should I be sorry for?

Richard   Nothing. Certainly not playing a record.

Jenny   What? Oh, you mean Kevin? You can't possibly be serious.

Richard   Why not? You've been flirting with him all afternoon. At the funeral.

Jenny   He lives next *door*.

Richard   That didn't stop you before.

Jenny   Everything's different now.

Richard   Is it? Is it really?

Jenny   You know it is. We both agreed to change. We made a deal.

Richard   I gave up being a boring accountant, and you gave up cheating on me. Was that the deal?

Jenny   (Once, *once*, for fuck's sake Richard, am I never gonna hear the fucking end of it?) The deal was, we would be a team, we would work together, we would fight the good fight. We would have the adventure of our lives.

Richard   Our marriage. Our future. 51st State.

Jenny   Yes.

Richard *moves the laptop to wipe beneath it, finds the letter.*

Richard (*to us*)   I nearly stopped there. I didn't want all this. Certainly not today. But then I opened the letter – by mistake, it was addressed to Jenny, but it was from the bank – and read: 'Dear Ms Ryan, RE: Standing order number blah, wish to advise, not been paid for six months due to lack of available funds, account number blah gravely in arrears, full amount must be paid immediately . . .' You've been using the mortgage account.

Jenny   I know. (*Short pause.*) I'm sorry.

Richard   I don't believe it.

Jenny   The money had to come from somewhere. How do you think we got all that material, for free? And pay the staff. And throw parties. And all the rest.

Richard   Why are you so calm? We're six months behind in our mortgage. We have no money to pay it. We have no money to pay for anything, I could barely buy a round of drinks today, at least my mother left the money for her own funeral . . . oh.

Jenny   What?

Richard   Oh Jesus Christ.

Jenny   *What?*

Richard   I get it.

Jenny   Get what?

Richard   You made a . . . a calculation, didn't you? Based on, um, a future inheritance.

Jenny   I wouldn't put it as clinically as that.

Richard   Wouldn't you? How would you put it then?

Jenny   Well, all right. I figured it should enter our plans at an earlier stage than it usually might.

Richard   Some might say, decently might. But I suppose you would say, almost anything is justified, in the adventure of our lives.

Jenny   Almost anything, yes.

Richard   My mother's house.

Jenny   Yes. Sorry, Richard, but you were paralysed. By the time we'd get it, we'd have lost our business. Lost our dream.

Pause.

Richard   We're not going to get it.

Jenny   What?

Richard   We're not going to inherit my mother's house.

Jenny   What do you mean? You're the only child.

Richard   She knew I was doing really well. And that I would never be reckless with money. I'm too level-headed for that. So she left the house to the Musicians' Benevolent Society.

Jenny   She what?

Richard   The will was drawn up years ago. So we are not getting that house, and we're going to lose this one, so on top of losing our jobs, and having no money, and being six figures in debt, we have nowhere to live.

Jenny   Oh my God.

Richard   And it's all your fucking fault. You . . . on the day of my mother's funeral, you thoughtless fucking, selfish fucking . . .

Jenny *sinks to the floor, weeping.*

Richard (*to us*)   And there was so much more I could have said: not just about her getting pissed drunk at my mother's funeral; or about how shallow and mediocre 51st State actually was, how it was all just overhyped, modish millennial bullshit with no, for all that on the Internet they call it content, no *content*, no depth, no *substance*; not just that, but about how Jenny had never finished a damn thing in her life, an arts degree, a catering diploma, careers in journalism, dance, fashion design, nursery teaching God help us, how she lacked the will, the concentration, the *character* to follow a damn thing through; how she desperately wanted attention, status, acclaim, while lacking the one thing that might have earned them: talent. I could have told her all that. I wanted to, I so fucking wanted to. But she couldn't have borne it. I looked at her, slumped there, weeping – for herself, I know, I know, in pity for herself, still, weeping nonetheless – and I knew I couldn't do it. How we worked was, she agreed to put up with me. If I told her how second-rate I knew she was – but how could I tell her that? I loved her too much. And for her to know I loved her in spite of so much . . . I knew she couldn't have borne it. So I hunkered down beside her, and I held her as she wept, and we sat there, the adventure of our lives in ruins around us.

Kevin   Two hundred years ago they began to quarry the granite to build the harbour of refuge out in the bay. And now, no one can remember a time when the slopes of the hill were intact, or when the church still stood proud at its peak, and the tolling of its bell called the villagers up to

Mass. They poured the granite into the sea, and the silver-
grey walls surged out of the blue water, like the outspread
wings of some great grey bird, and everything changed for
ever.

What happened was, one of the stoneworkers found a
collection of old Viking coins, all solid gold, buried in the
hills in a box the size and shape of a child's coffin. Now, the
fellow who found the fortune was Spanish, and there was
talk that his wife was some kind of witch, and that she had
directed, by consulting the moon and the stars, where he
should dig. So a number of the quarrymen went to see this
woman, who certainly looked the part, with her long black
hair and dark flashing eyes, and they asked her if there was
more treasure to be found, and she told them, simply, yes,
there was fortune enough for all if they knew where to look,
and if they wanted it badly enough. Soon every mason and
miner and stoneworker had abandoned the quarry and was
digging for treasure, and word soon spread far and wide
that gold had been found, and that more was to be had, and
an encampment of treasure seekers sprang up.

Now every dawn brought prospectors swarming all over the
hill, digging and raking, hacking back the gorse, burrowing
under yew and cypress trees, breaking down stone walls,
working without cease until the sun set behind the darkened
church. And although nobody actually found any gold, few
doubted that gold would once again be discovered.

And then one night, at twilight, a terrible shrieking and
wailing was heard, and as the treasure seekers flocked to the
commotion they saw smoke rising, and then, suddenly, a
flash of red light on the church walls, and – for a split-
second, or a few seconds, or a full minute, depending on
whose account you believe – there appeared what all
subsequently described as a Crucifix of Fire, glowing
brilliantly, screaming horribly, and then collapsing in a
tangled black ball of smoke and flame. And, just as the
money changers in the temple once fled the blazing anger of

Jesus Christ, the prospectors turned and ran in terror at the sight of this Crucifix of Fire, this flaming cross.

What happened was, some medical students, among the few to doubt the existence of the treasure, had taken four cats, and drugged them, and tied them together, and soaked them in paraffin, and tied Roman candles to their tails, and set them alight.

What happened was, God, disgusted at His children's greed and credulity, their naive belief that fortunes were lying about, waiting to be found by any idiot who cared to look, showed them a sign of His blazing power. And, like the women at the tomb when they saw that Christ's body had vanished, they were afraid.

What happened was, the quarrymen returned to their task, and the silver-grey walls of the harbour surged out of the blue water like the outspread wings of some great grey bird, and the hill was quarried out until its slopes resembled a cathedral.

Marion *and* **Kevin**.

Marion   Kevin finished his gold-rush story, but by that time, of course, 51st State had fallen apart.

Kevin   Which, I suppose, was the moral of the story all along.

Marion   Sometimes he'd go to Mass, but most days were spent up the hill.

Kevin   Thomas would come with me. We liked it up there.

Marion   We passed the children back and forth between us. We had run out of words. Silent days, and grey, as if the sky itself were hewn from granite.

Kevin   The vaulted cliffs of the quarry, like a cathedral. The Crucifix of Fire. The ruined church above us all.

Marion   I couldn't stop thinking of money. How were we going to live?

Kevin   How must we live? Mark's Gospel doesn't really end with Jesus telling the apostles to go forth and spread the word of God, with Jesus ascending into heaven and sitting at his father's right hand. Someone added that stuff in. No, what happens is, the women come to the tomb and the stone has been rolled away, and an angel is there, and he tells them Jesus of Nazareth is risen. Then Mark says: 'And they went out quickly, and fled from the sepulchre; for they trembled and were amazed; neither said they any thing to any man; for they were afraid.' That's all. And one scholar says the more accurate version is: 'They were scared, you see.' That the tomb was empty, that Jesus is gone, that He has left us, alone. 'They were scared, you see.'

Jenny *and* **Richard**.

Richard   We camped in my mother's house until the estate was sorted. Just held on tight for a while. Hiding from creditors. Covers over our heads.

Jenny   Eventually, I was sleeping sixteen hours a day. It was like being back at university. Except for being paralysed with misery, and fear, and shame.

Richard   We even helped tidy up the place for the sale. Our own house had been repossessed, and sold in the same week, for . . . for –

Jenny   Don't. Don't even think about it.

Marion *sits with a cup of coffee. Enter* **Kevin**.

Marion   And then a crack came in the granite sky.

Kevin   See you later.

Marion   Is Thomas outside?

Kevin   He's showing Mrs Patterson his bucket and spade.

Pause.

Marion   You look well.

Kevin   I went for a swim.

Marion   You did not.

Kevin   Down at Whitestrand. The rocky cove.

Marion   Was it freezing?

Kevin   It was . . . bracing. Spring tide. Waves crashing over my head. Felt good.

Marion   And then Mass?

Kevin   No.

Marion   No?

Kevin   Then breakfast. I was starving.

Pause.

Marion   So where are you going with Thomas, up the hill again?

Kevin   He has his bucket and spade. The sun is shining, and we're going to the beach.

Marion   You're going to the beach.

Kevin   Yes. Is that all right?

Marion   Sure. Absolutely. Just, you haven't been much for going to the beach recently. Type of thing.

Kevin   The sun hasn't been shining much recently.

Marion   The sun isn't actually shining today, Kevin.

Kevin   I know. But it's threatening. Tomorrow, or the day after.

Marion   The day after tomorrow.

Kevin   Type of thing. (*Pause.*) So. See you later?

Marion   We'll be here.

Richard *and* **Jenny**.

Richard   And then gradually, we began to . . .

Jenny   Pick ourselves up. We rented a flat. It's not very
. . . well, everywhere's so expensive nowadays.

Richard   It's a studio apartment.

Jenny   It's a bedsit.

Richard   Above a late-night kebab shop.

Jenny   But with a little scrub-up, and a little paint . . .

Richard   Accountancy doesn't like risk-takers. It's not
what the profession is about. Trying to explain a year-long
gap in my résumé would have been tricky at the best of
times; telling an interview panel I had spent it pouring all
my money down the toilet, well, it wasn't a good argument
for why I should be controlling anyone else's finances. So
long-term, it wasn't a solution. But what else could we do?

Jenny   I could cook. I was always able to cook.

Richard   She could, actually, really well. Those gourmet
sandwiches used to be bloody good.

Jenny   I started it up again myself: there were offices near
where the new flat was. I leafleted them, and built up some
orders, and got the gourmet sandwich business back on the
road.

Richard   I was impressed. It went like a bomb. I thought,
what about evening meals? Lot of hungry people now with
no time to waste in the kitchen.

Jenny   I wouldn't have had the nerve to suggest it.

Richard   We have all this technical expertise. Pity to
waste it. Because everything in business, even failure –
especially failure – everything is an opportunity. I really
believe that.

Jenny   So we have a new website. Called Suppertime.
It's –

Richard   There's a range of starters, main courses and
puddings, all displayed on the site: photographs of the
dishes, all the ingredients listed, you can choose for a quiet
night in or a dinner party, it's up to you.

Jenny   Richard, stop selling. It's basically a –

Richard   And I deliver all the food, ready to eat. When
we expand, we hope to have a fleet of delivery . . . agents.
But at the moment –

Jenny   Basically an upmarket pizza delivery service. We
have printed menus too.

Richard   I drop one off with every order.

Jenny   Mostly, people don't bother with the website. They
just order over the phone.

Richard   So I think it's safe to say, we've bounced back.

Jenny   Well. We're still bouncing.

Richard   On top of which –

Jenny   Go on then.

Richard   Jenny stopped drinking.

Jenny   I meant about the baby, Richard.

Richard   I just thought it was worth mentioning –

Jenny   I wouldn't be drinking anyway, would I, being
pregnant?

Richard   That you had reached a decision –

Jenny   No.

Richard   About your drinking –

Jenny   No, Richard, just *no*!

Pause.

Richard   Yes, we've bounced back all right. Ready to face the future again.

Jenny   I suppose . . . I suppose we're lucky, when it comes down to it. Relative to . . . I mean, God help poor Marion. No one saw that coming.

Richard   First NPK, and then Kevin.

Jenny   No one really knows what happened.

Richard   I had to identify the body.

Marioin *and* **Kevin**.

Marion   He jumped.

Kevin   I had Thomas in the buggy; if I were going to kill myself, would I have brought him along?

Marion   He was going to take Thomas with him. He was going to kill his own son. Like one of those cases you read about in the newspapers.

Kevin   Jesus Christ Almighty.

Marion   Thomas was the one he really loved: that's what I couldn't understand about it.

Kevin   Because I didn't jump, I fell. I slipped.

Marion   The child in the buggy, alone up there for eight hours.

Kevin   He fell asleep. He was fine, actually.

Marion   I wouldn't see the body. I got Richard to identify him.

Kevin   It was chance.

Marion   It was fate.

Kevin   Whatever.

Marion   There is a difference.

Richard   I think Marion was convinced it was suicide at first.

Marion   He had become obsessed: the ruined church, the Crucifix of Fire, he kept talking about the end of St Mark's Gospel.

Jenny   How could he though, with two beautiful little children?

Richard   I said: don't mention any of that, depression, religious mania, and not a word of suicide. Money worries strictly short-term, pensionable job waiting for him at a leading school. Devoted father, had his son with him, last thing he would have done would be to expose Thomas to any danger.

Marion   A tragic accident.

Richard   His life was insured, wasn't it? Of course it was, standard terms of the mortgage.

Marion   I got the house. Own it now, outright. So all I have to do –

Kevin   Is look after the little ones.

Richard   It might have been the best outcome. Tragic situation, but maybe for the best.

Marion   And then I began to wonder. Perhaps that's how it happened. Kevin, seeing no other way out, contrived to kill himself, but make it look like an accident. Knowing suicide would void the policy.

Kevin   I didn't know suicide would void the policy.

Marion   An act of love. A sacrifice for his family. Almost Christlike in its selflessness –

Kevin   Oh, go on then. If it makes it any easier to live with.

Marion   Maybe that's how it happened. Although it doesn't make it any easier to live with.

Richard   And then one night we had a major order for
Killiney. Full dinner party, starters, mains and puddings for
sixteen. Big production number, Jenny was up at dawn. But
we made it. We weren't in the business of failure any more,
that's what I'd say to her. It was only when I came through
the gate – eucalyptus and palm trees lined the drive, gravel
crunched as I pulled up by the Jags and Mercs, back garden
ran down to the shore – only when I rang the bell, only
when the door opened that I realised whose house it was. A
maid – in a uniform – stood in the hallway. Filipina, I think
she was, or Mexican. She took the food, and asked me to
wait. There was a hubbub of voices from the front room. I
could make out Michael's voice, and Gerry's laugh. I hadn't
seen either of them for ages. They didn't know about the
new business. I was sure there were other people I'd been at
university with at the party as well. The whole thing
sounded so familiar. After a few moments, the maid
appeared at the far end of the hall. Michael's wife was with
her. Caroline.

Jenny   Annabel.

Richard   Annabel, that's right. I nodded, and began to
smile. But she looked right through me. Then she turned
quickly, and disappeared back into the party. She came out
again and gave an envelope to the Mexican or Filipina
maid. The maid walked down the hall and handed me the
envelope, and thanked me, and I smiled and nodded and
left. As I went down the steps and crunched across the
gravel drive towards my car, I could feel people looking out
the front window at me. I didn't look round.

Jenny   In the envelope, there was a cheque for the food,
and a tip for two hundred pounds. In cash.

Richard   I sent the tip back.

Jenny   I heard him lying awake that night. He was crying.

Richard   I wasn't looking for anyone's pity. We only had
ourselves to blame. And . . . and business . . . business is

such a flexible, such a *hospitable* system . . . no sooner had it knocked us out than it was letting us bounce right back. What more could you ask for?

Jenny   Richard's grandfather had been a small-holding tenant, on a big estate somewhere down the country. His father had been in the civil service. And owned his own house. And Richard had made it to university. So the idea that instead of moving up –

Richard   There I was, left waiting in the hall, like some fucking . . . like their fucking . . .

Jenny   We were going to have a baby. Maybe we weren't paying our debts, but we could pay our way. We *had* bounced back. We were looking towards the future.

Kevin   'They were scared, you see.'

Marion   And then I remembered the last time I saw Kevin. How he'd just been for a swim, how he looked . . . *glowing*. Like he'd been brought back to life. See you later, he said. (*Pause.*) I can't look up at the ruined church now. I can't stand the sight of it any more.

Kevin   Look the other way then. I told you. Look in the Pattersons' window. Watch them dance.

Marion   On Saturday nights, Mr and Mrs Patterson get all dressed up, and they dance to the old tunes. Waltz, quickstep, slow foxtrot. They're still good dancers. They don't smile too much, and they don't exactly work up a sweat. They just seem so easy with each other. Like they were meant to be.

Jenny   Some places just feel like home. You sense it, instantly. Home at last. That was what it felt like up there, in the shadow of the rock.

We're on a defaulters' list now. Chances are, we'll never get a mortgage again. Even if they'd let us have one, I can't see how we could afford it, we've that many debts. Richard says

we will. But I think he just says that to help me feel better.
Because of course, it was my fault we were flung out.

God, though, I'd give anything to make it back there. To
have had it once and seen it taken away is so much worse
than never to have known it at all. If there was just some
way we could get back home.

Richard   We thought that it was finished. But history was
never finished. The past was never over. We hoped that it
was, that we had put all the old wounds behind us by
dreaming hard of the future, by holding fast to Now, but
history is part of now, and part of our future, and look, here
it comes again, a tide at the bidding of some strange,
capricious moon – it seems to stay out for ever, and the
shore is paved over, and much building is done, consecrated
to the Future, Temples of Modernity – and then the tide
turns, and history crashes back in again, challenging
anything new to stand its ground if it can, and if it isn't
strong enough, to be swept away.

Marion   Aimee published Kevin's gold-rush story as a
'Times Gone By' feature. A few weeks later, they reprinted
his poem. I have them both framed, hanging on the wall.
For the children.

Kevin
'My boy was barely fifteen minutes old,
When Death walked through the door and spoke my
name,
And touched my face (his hand, of course, was cold)
And said, "It's not for you or yours I came,
I'm here for the stillborn in the next room,
Just thought I'd drop by, say a quick hello,
Your wife and son are fine, they'll thrive and bloom,
But you and me, we'd better get to know
One another." "Promise me this," I said,
"Promise you'll take me first. I couldn't bear
To live, knowing my little boy was dead."
"No promises," said Death, "I'm in your care,

As much as you're in mine." The baby slept;
I held Death in my arms, and smiled, and wept.'

Marion   There's a cold wind blowing down from the hill. Cold against the glass, cold enough to make you shiver. I'll keep the little ones in bed with me. Keep us . . . please keep us all . . . safe and warm tonight.

Music: 'Alone Together' – Jo Stafford

The light changes.

Above, the ruined church spire casts its shadow on **Richard** *and* **Jenny** *and* **Kevin** *and* **Marion***, as the music plays.*

The light fades slowly to darkness.

By the same author

Declan Hughes Plays : 1